Pastoral Scene in the West Indies

[*From a lithograph by J. B. Kidd.*

WEST INDIAN SUMMER

A RETROSPECT

by

JAMES POPE-HENNESSY

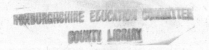
LONDON
B. T. BATSFORD LTD.
15 NORTH AUDLEY STREET, W.1

TO CLARISSA AT FONTAINEBLEAU

First Published, Summer 1943

36017

MADE AND PRINTED IN GREAT BRITAIN

FOREWORD

THIS IS NOT a travel-book but a book about travellers. It sets out to tell again the published experiences of nine English visitors to the West Indies. Some of these travellers—Raleigh, Trollope, Froude—were famous men ; others—Waller, Henry Coleridge, Mrs. Carmichael—were little known in their own day and may well have been utterly forgotten since. Two of them lived in the sixteenth century, one in the seventeenth century, the remainder under George III, George IV and Queen Victoria. These sketches are chiefly designed to illustrate the reactions of strangers to West Indian ways of life as well as to the sumptuous scenery of the Caribbean islands during the last three hundred years. The book's aim, in fact, is as limited as its scope.

Until 1939 life in the English colonies was much what it had always been—busy, patriotic, traditional, but conducted in an atmosphere tinged with incongruity and a sense of exile. The narratives in this volume do not presuppose any detailed knowledge of English colonies in general or the West Indies in particular. It is enough to remember that these islands form an arc that stretches from the coasts of Florida to those of Venezuela and contains the Gulf of Mexico and the Caribbean Sea. They belong variously to the British, the Dutch, the French and the Americans. One tends to forget, however, the great multitude of these West Indies (the Virgins alone comprise more than a hundred islets), peaks of a submerged mountain range. Geographically the Antilles fall into three groups : the Bahamas, the Greater Antilles (Cuba, Jamaica, Haiti, Porto Rico) and the Lesser Antilles. The Lesser Antilles themselves subdivide into the Windward Group—St. Lucia and all islands south of it—and the Leewards, those islands to its north. This is all the knowledge of the West Indies that the book assumes in its reader ; this, and a recollection that Barbados, Jamaica, Nevis, St. Kitts and Dominica have been English since the seventeenth century,

Trinidad since the close of the eighteenth ; that Guadaloupe and Martinique have always been French ; that St. Thomas, now American, was once a colony of Denmark.

It has been the fate of the West Indies to suffer from what might be termed the Eldorado *motif*. In the sixteenth century they were important as actual stepping stones to this mythical kingdom, supposed to lie concealed behind the swamps of the American continent. They were incidentally objects of ambition for their rich fisheries of pearls. In the next two hundred years they became, in a sense, Eldorados on their own—little paradises of sugar plantations, free labour and huge, swiftly-made fortunes. In the nineteenth century politics and economics combined to ruin the islands' trade. British-owned plantations stood weed-infested, white colonial houses became mildewed and decayed, towns were as dirty and ill-conditioned as those described by Trollope and Froude. Since Slave Emancipation two factors have done something to renew the importance of the West Indies—the opening of the Panama Canal and the discovery of oil. In the present war the islands have come back into the news as bases to be leased for American defence.

The historical essays in this book are meant to be accurate, but they are held together by episodes that are largely fictional. Although I did myself serve as a temporary aide-de-camp to one of Trinidad's most distinguished governors during some dank summer months in 1939, it is only just to explain that the central figure of this book is not in intention myself. It would be disingenuous to deny that my Trinidad experiences suggested these sketches ; but the modern episodes and the contemporary judgments they contain are not altogether authentic nor wholly true.

Apart from this short stay in Trinidad I have another connection with the West Indies, for my Irish grandfather John Pope-Hennessy (original for Trollope's character of Phineas Finn) was Governor of Barbados in the Federation Riots of 1876, an outbreak notorious in local history. My grandfather was not liked by the white community, who suspected him (with justice) of sympathy with negro rights.

On a petition from the planters of the island he was called home. Should this little book, then, ever reach a Barbadian reader he may rest assured that the few harsh references he may find in it to his island or its inhabitants are perfectly deliberate. This is, in any case, all that Barbadians would expect from someone who has liked living in Trinidad : for the rivalry between these two islands is as bitter as their scenery is contrasting. It is but one example of that exciting individualism that makes the West Indies what they are.

29 *December* 1942,
Ladbroke Grove, London

NOTE

The portraits in this book have been selected with the aid of Mr. C. M. Hake, Director of the National Portrait Gallery. Those in the Gallery are published with his permission. The Lely picture of Elizabeth, Duchess of Albemarle, at Welbeck Abbey is reproduced by the kindness of the Duke of Portland, who has allowed the portrait to be photographed. A number of the engravings of West Indian scenes are owned by Messrs. W. T. Spencer of New Oxford Street, whose assistant Miss Watkins has been most helpful. All the illustrations are intended to bear a special relation to the text, and to suggest the atmosphere of the West Indies.

CONTENTS

Chapter One

THE BOTANIC GARDEN

1939

> The sun's rim dips ; the stars rush out ;
> At one stride comes the dark.
>
> CaCoLERIDGE

ANOTHER DAY WAS over. Cashel watched its close from a hilltop above Port of Spain. He stood in a small clearing upon the hilltop, a place from which the tropical shrubs had been hacked away to show the view. The hill was high and steep, one of the chain that rises north and east of Port of Spain, excluding wind and air from that hot city. A dusty yellow motor-road twists to the summit, and here and there along the roadside sit bungalows in garden-plots that are bright with bougainvillea and spiky canna blooms.

You would not have known that this was an evening in June. As he looked down the hill Cashel thought of the damp heat that lies perpetually across the city, the savannah and the whole island of Trinidad. Far below him he could see Government House, an L-shaped building that from up here seemed made of painted tin. At one end of Government House a tower like a box carried a flagpole with a limp imperial flag. East of " G.H." another large white building, the Insane Asylum, lay shrouded in dark trees. To the west stretched the sere Savannah, encircled by the houses of the well-to-do. Beyond the Savannah is the city of Port of Spain, burned out in 1813 and replanned upon the grid system, with fine rectangular boulevards and an adequate number of slums. In the twilight the city began to look beautiful. Naked flares flamed in the streets of the Indian quarter. Soon the houses down there would be glowing with oil-lamps, and pungent with the smell of greasy Indian cooking ; shambling negro figures would cast shadows on the peeling house-walls as they passed. Beyond the city streets the outline of the harbour was becoming indistinct. The mild expanses of the brown Caroni Swamp were blurred. Beyond the harbour and the swamp heaved the waters of the Gulf of Paria, thick with silt from the Orinoco delta where the scarlet ibis nests among the mangrove roots. Beyond the Gulf of Paria the huge mountains of the continent hid the last flare-up of the setting sun.

Cashel sighed. He glanced once more at the placid Gulf and started to pick his way slowly down a footpath beside Lady Chancellors Road. He often came up here to watch the sunset. Hating the fierce sunlight that beat upon the lawns and the verandahs, and sizzled the tarmac round Government House, he liked to see the sun go down, dropping behind the jagged skyline of Venezuela across the way. Cashel also loathed the objects the sun encouraged—the tough flowers, the giant butterflies that flopped over the dry lawns, the magenta bougainvillea in the gardens, the pink and orange poui trees that flamed along the hills. He thought of a northern landscape and of a London sky.

Following the path downhill, Cashel reached the entrance to the Botanic Garden. Passing through a wicket gate, and skirting a mildewed octagonal pavilion and some brittle clusters of bamboo, he emerged into an avenue of bay-rum trees. There were thirty-two of these trees, sixteen a side ; their trunks were tall and even, and their bark was as smooth as taut skin. After crossing two gravel paths, and avoiding a cage in which baskets of orchid plants like headhunters' trophies were hanging in tidy rows, he plunged into an artificial gulley. At one end of this gulley (which was strewn with rocks and tufted with jaunty ferns), grew a giant Indian Saman tree. Beneath the ragged shade of this great tree, and all amongst the rattling palm-leaves, was the cottage in which Cashel now lived.

The A.D.C.'s cottage was a complicated building of tarred wood. It was of the chalet-type, with fretwork gables, more doors than windows, and a miniature verandah on two sides. The back door opened on to a swimming pool which, though protected by a roof of rabbit-wire, was ordinarily littered with flower-petals and the bodies of flying ants. The branches of the Saman seemed to overshadow the whole building, and its long parasite creepers would tap mournfully against the window-frames of Cashel's bedroom. The persistence of these creepers would sometimes awaken him (he lived alone). Once woken it was not easy to get to sleep. Frogs croaked, cicadas tittered in the garden. Twigs splashed into the swimming-pool. Heavy objects fell with a thud in the nearby gulley. On some nights it was even possible to fancy that heavy cautious footsteps were trampling round and round the little house. In distant Port of Spain a dog howled : occasionally a more curious cry would come wafted on the night air from the lunatic asylum in St. Anne's. On such nights Cashel would lean from his bedroom window and peer into the Botanic Garden, at the swaying creepers on the boughs of the Saman, each strand clearly visible in the metal-blue moonlight.

Cashel had grown very fond of his cottage, and of the gulley, Nutmeg Ravine, in the Botanic Garden. They both exemplified the Victorian romanticism which had come to seem the main appeal of the Caribbean. There is a mid-nineteenth century feeling about the whole of Trinidad. It's not merely the buildings and their gardens (most of which were indeed designed under Victorian influences) ; it is something you can sense even in the High Woods, those rank forests that clothe the hills in the north and centre of the island, and which are intersected only by a few perilous motoring roads. Up in the High Woods grows matted foliage of every shade of green, lit here and there superbly by the orange sheaves of wild poinsettia flower called Pride of Trinidad, or by the garish orchids that ride many feet up on the boughs of the trees. In its brilliance, and its shiny detail, the tropical forest reminded him of the enamelled qualities of minor pre-Raphaelite art.

It was on the way to Port of Spain when the boat lay off Bridgetown in Barbados that Cashel had seen his first tropical trees. There in the long walled garden of another Government House grew cannon-ball trees and calabash trees, cabbage palms, and cluster upon cluster of bamboo. The trees threw heavy shadows across the lawns and pathways,

over the beds of red and blue flowers, over the negro gardeners
in their white cotton coats. This garden seemed to him a
lithograph of the 'sixties brought to life. The house, on the
other hand, conformed closely to Cashel's previous illusions
about the West Indian colonies. It is a well-proportioned
eighteenth century building, low and white, with windows
curved against the buffeting insistence of the warm, perpetual
Barbados gale, a big cruciform drawing-room, a portico,
clattering jalousies, and chandeliers in which each separate
candle-flame is protected by a vase of glass. It seems severed
from its garden by at least one hundred and fifty years.

As he gazed upon this garden Cashel realised how the
Victorian interest in the odd and the excessive found its ideal
object in tropical foliage. He understood the vogue of the
conservatory and of the glass-house. It was easy to picture
English visitors of the 'fifties strolling entranced about this
very garden, wondering idly at much that their pale Barbadian
hosts would take for granted—the cabbage palms towering
above them, the calabash and the trumpet trees, the giant canna
blossoms, the brilliance of bougainvillea seen at last in its
proper setting, the white stephanotis against the blood-red
hibiscus hedge, the swish of the humming-birds darting, the
long, long ropes of creeper looped wildly about the high trees.
All around them would echo the shrill, sad repetition of
tropical birds' cries, and towards evening the fireflies, those
nightly miracles, would flash and sparkle over the lawns in the
early darkness. From the windows of their bedrooms the
Governor's guests would lean out for their first glimpse of the
Barbadian moon. Frogs would be croaking in the scented
garden, and the palm-trees would look gaunt and silly under
the stars, like fur hats stuck up on poles. In the morning
after waking to the muslin world of the great mosquito nets—
the sunshine knife-like through the louvres, making striped
patterns on the floor—they would descend to breakfast in the
submarine gloom of the dining-room, where liveried negroes
waited and the plate glimmered on the sideboards. Later the
visitors would be taken driving past the clustering houses and
huts of the suburbs, out through the cane-fields, the yam

plots and the fields of guinea corn, beneath the bread-fruit trees and the ceibas, over the undulating dusty roads or along the white sea-shore to Speights Town, a track so covered by the coral sand that the carriage wheels often stuck fast and the carriage jolted to a standstill in the heat. In Barbados, as in all the islands, there was the constant emphasis for strangers on the unexpected, the wonderful ; the tree, for example, which grew behind Mr. Foster Clerk's house in Bridgetown " in a serpentine form upon the surface of the ground " and which looked like a colossal dragon. At the foot of a glen in Turner's Hall Wood, on Sir Henry FitzHerbert's land, was another phenomenon : a gaseous pool that could be lit with a candle and would then " shoot upwards in a quivering column of light."

All this and more Cashel had learned from the journals of nineteenth century travellers which his friend the archbishop had lent him. What he had read he used to turn over and over in his mind, brooding upon each incident, each piece of descriptive writing, until these past visitors came to seem his companions. He thought he saw their tight silhouettes upon the iron verandahs of Government House ; he imagined them as they stepped gaily from their steam-propelled yachts into the harbour-master's launches ; he imagined bearded officials bowing to Lady Brassey and hand-picked guests greeting Prince Henry of Battenberg amidst the tubs of croton-leaves. At twilight in Trinidad, in the Botanic Gardens, their presence seemed all around him : they swarmed and whispered in the swiftly gathering darkness, men with binoculars and malacca canes, women with parasols and bonnets and bustles. Nutmeg Ravine was full of them, wandering hither and thither, uttering sharp cries of delight as they peered upwards at the orchids, pointing to the screw-pines, the oil-palms and the talipots, asking the names of the Panama Hat Plant and the dignified Ivory Palm. Cashel liked to consider where they had come from and where they were going. From Madeira via Barbados perhaps ; and probably they would steam out through the Trinidad Bocas, by Tobago and the Grenadines, along the green volcanic coastline of Martinique, past the

Pithons of St. Lucia, following the chain of the pretty, neglected Caribbee islands, those smooth wooded contours, those leaning palm-trees and white sea beaches, that deep translucent water filled with black and purple fish. In his mind's eye Cashel watched the yachts as they dwindled on the night horizon, beneath the South Atlantic sky (a thin trail of phosphorescence churning in the propeller's wake), passing away forever with their smug, sad world.

Cashel sighed again. A pallid boy of twenty-two, he neither looked nor felt like anybody's aide-de-camp. His meditative face, large eyes and curly hair, reminded you of a Bulwer-Lytton hero, but failed to inspire confidence in a Crown Colony. His low voice and remote manner, which passed unnoticed in Europe, seemed markedly eccentric in Trinidad. He hated answering the telephone and ordering the car. Official life oppressed and bewildered him. He turned from the empty darkness of the Botanic Garden and entering his cottage, shut the door.

Chapter Two

THE TRAVELLING POSTMASTER
1858

Old Trollope banging about the world.
FROUDE

IN THE BIG ballroom of Government House they were doing the Palais Glide. The band played the bold tune boldly. Lines of dancers, their arms linked round each others' waists, kicked a leg forward and took a step back, kicked forward, stepped back, swinging down the room. There were dresses of shot-silk, of plain muslin, of linen, of chiffon with gay patterns ; orchis sprays fastened with diamond paste clips— white orchids with scarlet freckles, violet flowers with gaping mouths, strange ochre flowers with black stamen from the flowershops down in Port of Spain. Gilt buttons shimmered on the uniforms of the colonial police. The smooth heads of the midshipmen were tousled with exertion, their faces pinker from the heat. Up and down, round and round, up and down—it really seemed as if they would never stop. It was the last dance of the evening, and the grins of the negro band had become empty and fixed. The dance went on. Feet pounded heavily upon the chalked parquet floor.

All along one side of the ballroom the high French windows were open. Against the spaces of wall between each pair of windows standard fans buzzed, discharging spirals of draught. Six bars of light from the windows fell across the iron verandahs, glinting on the whiskey tumblers and on the varnished legs of wicker tables. People giggled, chairs scraped on the verandahs. The tip of a cigarette glowed orange and dimmed. Ice chinked.

In a far corner of the verandah, away from the din, sat Cashel in a linen dinner jacket. He was staring out on to the lawns that lay clear but colourless in the moonlight. A curl of stephanotis clung about the ironwork of the balustrade in front of him, and out in the formal garden croton plants turned their polished leaves with indifference to the stars. There was a small, an awkward urn in the centre of the formal garden. The paths that radiated from the urn were just ever so slightly out of truth.

All round this house, thought Cashel, rise the palm-trees and the samans. He saw the building as a white shell of noise and light, ringed about by the tall royal palms. From the hillside now it must seem a glowing lantern. Slowly in his own mind he assembled the bird's-eye view—the low white house with its lawns and flower-beds about it, the Botanic Gardens a tangle of guinea grass and monstrous trees, the Savannah wan in the moonlight making a pale contrast to the masses of the hills. He thought of the High Woods that clothe the hills, and of the deserted cocoa plantations— rickety houses, spindly shrub and elegant purple pods—that he had seen in the valleys between. He thought last of the whole island of Trinidad and of the surrounding sea in the starlight, and of the breakers that hurl spray and coloured sea-shells on to the Northern Shore at Blanchisseuse.

The music stopped. His thoughts were jolted back into reality. As he rose he dropped his dancing-card, with its scarlet pencil attached by a white-tassled thread ; he stooped to pick it up, and people began to move past him quickly, making for the cars which lay huddled round the main entrance like a clump of mussels round a rock.

" Oh, you goose," said the fast Jamaican lady, " don't you know what quick dances are ? I never dance anything but quick dances, quadrilles are so deadly dull."

She was speaking to Anthony Trollope in the year 1858. Quick dances he soon discovered were the schottische, the polka and the galopade. At first local expressions in Jamaica were eminently confusing, but he got used to them after a time. " Will you have a long drink or a short one ? " It sounded odd but it was very practical ; and like Froude when introduced to " cocktail " in Bridgetown, Barbados, Trollope quickly realised the necessity in this torpid climate of such

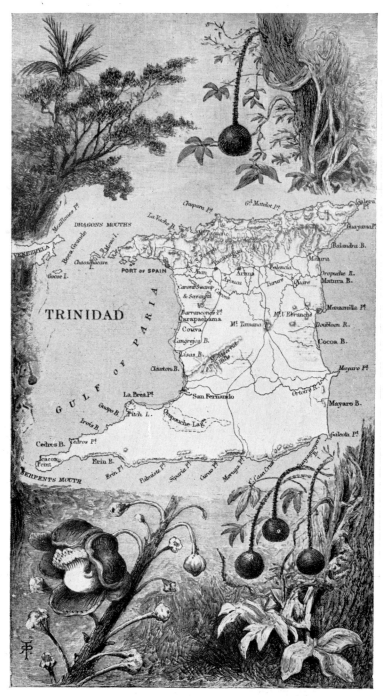

[*From Lady Brassey's " In the Trades, the Tropics and the Roaring 'Forties "*
Decorative Map of Trinidad, 1885

[*From the portrait by Samuel Laurence in the National Portrait Gallery.*

Anthony Trollope in 1865

occasional drinks. Like all his contemporaries who visited the West Indian islands, Trollope was disappointed by the food if pleased by the drink. One of his predecessors, a lady who had landed in St. Vincent in 1820, had confessed herself much disgruntled by being offered preserved English rasp-berries for her very first meal on West Indian soil. Where were the guavas and the otaheite gooseberries ? the pine-apple and the paw-paw for which she pined ? Like her, Trollope was fed on tinned meats and tinned potatoes ; beef-steak and onions for breakfast ; oxtail soup ; cheese after every meal. Nothing, he perceived, was of value in the West Indies that did not come from " home."

It was in the late autumn of 1858 that Trollope bundled aboard the *Atrato* and sailed for the West Indies. His first port of call was St. Thomas (" a Niggery-Hispano-Dano-Yankee-doodle place "), where he changed boats and continued on to Kingston in Jamaica. Later experience of West Indian travel made him regret his contempt for the comforts of these earlier ships—the claret inadequately iced, the walnuts often rotten, the withering apples and the narrow berths. In future passages from one green island to another he found that to get any wines or fruit at all or a clean berth were rare luxuries in this part of the world. His journey to the West Indies, like most of the other journeys of his life, was occasioned by his job in the Post Office. Like all the other journeys it too resulted in a book. *Barchester Towers* had been scribbled in Irish railway carriages, *Dr. Thorne* finished on the way to Egypt to negotiate a postal treaty with the Pasha, and the journey to the Caribbean resulted in a straightforward travel diary which its author, many years afterwards, declared to be " on the whole . . . the best book that has come from my pen. It is," he adds, " short, and I think I may venture to say amusing, useful and true."

As he stepped ashore on the Danish island of St. Thomas, a negress dressed in white muslin pressed a rose into Trollope's hand. " That's for love, dear," she said to the burly English gentleman in steel spectacles. He promised that it should be, observing for his diary that she was a laundry-woman and that

2

she wore pink gloves. In its way it was a characteristic West Indian welcome : Trollope, jovial, bearded and bespectacled, was entering a sunlit and illogical world. He had already severed his connection with ordinary existence—the daily adjustments of the Irish postal system, the financial propositions of publishers, the hearty friendships of the hunting field : the postal expert had come to a society many of whose inhabitants prefer to carry their correspondence balanced upon the top of their heads, the novelist to a society in which the essentials of life—its sustenance, its most elementary comforts—bulk larger than manners, emotions or political intrigue. How far indeed were these casual island people (with their nasal twang and their sherry cobblers) from the chinking of Mrs. Proudie's teacups, or the cottage of Madame Max Goesler, abutting on Park Lane !

Kingston was the first town at which Trollope stayed in Jamaica. He detested it. On a map it looked deceptively perfect : in practice it was shoddy and half-built. There was no *trottoir*, no macademisation. There was not even any system for lighting up the streets. How badly it compared, he afterwards reflected, with even such a place as Cien Fuegos, or Havana, where oil-lamps and gas jets shone along the walls. Spanish Town seemed no better. Parched and deserted, it was empty of all life save an occasional negro lurching by in the glare of the sun, and droves of lean rapacious pigs that grovelled in the gutters. There were no good inns in Spanish Town—or as they were called no " lodging-houses." The opinion he began to form of British rule in the West Indies was low.

At the time of Trollope's visit Jamaica was in fact suffering under one of those periods of total stagnation to which even the most wealthy of the West Indies have been subject, and from which some of the less fortunate islands have never shaken free. Increasing poverty, bringing with it an exaggeration of class and colour hostility, had produced a state of melancholy and tension. In 1850 a visitation of Asiatic cholera decimated the population. The islanders began to despair. The poverty was partially due to the humanitari-

anism of contemporary England. Nineteen years before
Trollope's journey the slave emancipation in Jamaica had been
completed, and the heavy financial losses consequent upon
this measure, together with the results of Peel's abolition of
Protection, had not been properly counterbalanced by the
sudden introduction of 20,000 coolie labourers from India.
This cheap " indentured " labour was intended to supplement
the now erratic work of the freed negroes. But as Trollope
soon noticed the negroes regarded Emancipation not as freedom
from slavery merely, but as freedom from the silly necessity
for any regular work at all. The owners of the sugar estates,
who had lost £16 a head on each of their slaves, found their
managers faced with the refusal of Jamaican negroes to do
a hand's turn. It was an aggravating position. The slaves
now lay about beneath the bread-fruit trees in placid dis-
obedience, sucking segments of pomegranate and listlessly
explaining to estate managers that they had earned plenty of
money for that week. One after another the great estates fell
into neglect. Negroes began to " squat " upon plots of land
previously under cultivation and to which anyway they had no
vestige of right. The Europeans and Creoles, up to the
reign of William IV all too competent at dealing with Africans,
were baffled and powerless. The distrust and hatred Trollope
detected in the island in 1858 fermented for a further seven
years and then exploded in the famous riots of 1865 with their
aftermath, the Case of Governor Eyre. The riots were
alleged to have been caused by the indiscreet conduct of
George William Gordon, a coloured man of wealth and
position. Gordon was accused of negrophile sympathies and
his habit of addressing negro gatherings was strongly dis-
approved by the authorities. Accordingly he was held
responsible for a negro onslaught on the custos and vestry of
the parish of St. Thomas in the East one mild October afternoon, when many Europeans, including troops sent down to
guard the civilians, were killed. The Governor, Eyre,
proclaimed martial law ; Gordon was hanged ; hundreds of
negroes were flogged throughout the island and over a
thousand negro houses burned to the ground. But public

opinion in England, for long contented to ignore Jamaica, became suddenly aware of the riots. From awareness English people passed to indignation, and the indignation was directed against Governor Eyre. A Commission of Enquiry condemned the Governor's action and he was recalled to England. His name lingers in the West Indies as a legend, and a signal for controversy to this day.

. Trollope, who soon decided that he understood the negroes, did not trust them. The Creoles and Europeans he found amiable and uninteresting. The people he liked best, and to whom he felt that the future of the West Indies belonged, were the coloured people. They were then much as they are to-day—vital, intelligent, resilient. Sententiously he stated his conviction that " Providence has sent the white man and the black man to these regions in order that from them may spring a race fitted by intellect for civilisation ; and fitted also by physical organisation for tropical labour." He looked forward to the withdrawal of English officials from the West Indies, their task accomplished and their lessons taught. Just as Australia, just as Canada must and would detach themselves from the British Empire in the years to come, so he imagined these islands slipping away from their allegiance under the guidance of a coffee-coloured intelligentsia.

Trollope's was a liberal view, born of idealism but supported by a measure of observation. Already he perceived the " millstone " of white resistance in Jamaica to be permeated with the solvent of coloured social ambitions. Soon he thought it would become pumice stone and, crumbling, disappear. It was only in the last few years that the coloured women of Jamaica had begun to marry. Previously they had been honoured to be the mistresses of white men, privileged to bear their children. But now they had discovered that a marriage with one of their own stock need not exclude them from white society. " These people marry now," said a middle-aged lady to Anthony Trollope, " but their mothers and grandmothers never thought of looking to that at all. Are we to associate with the children of such women, and teach our daughters that vice is to be shunned ? " The echoes of the matronly voices of the 1850's persist in the West Indies to-day. The triumph of colour is not yet wholly accomplished.

One aspect of the coloured people, their fantastic affectations, fascinated Trollope. He was sitting peacefully in an hotel in Port Antonio one warm evening after dinner, when a young lady dressed in white stepped into the room. She was a coloured girl, wearing a crinoline and ribbons. Her black hair was elegantly brushed. Upon her fingers sparkled many rings. " Whence she came or who she was I did not know and never learnt. That she was familiar in the house I presume from her moving the books and little ornaments on the tables, and arranging the cups and shells upon a shelf. ' Heigh-ho,' she ejaculated when I had watched her for about half a minute." As she sighed again he spoke to her. Was she in sorrow ? " Sorrow enough," the young lady replied, " I'se in de deepest sorrow, heigh-ho me ! Well de world will end some day." She came and sat beside him on the sofa, striking one hand quickly upon another in a mannerism he had noticed frequently among the coloured women. " 'Tis a very bad world," she continued, " and sooner over de better. . . . My heart's clean broke, I know dat." The conversation, of which his record covers many pages, developed along these dispiriting lines. She was, it appeared, called Josephine (" do you like dat name ? ") and she had been loved and jilted by a Jew ; she was also a Baptist and frightened of being " read out " for this unChristian connection. Her immediate dilemma was that she had to return to her home in Kingston on a " droger " of which her Jew was Captain. With Trollope's help she reached a kind of solution of her difficulties. As they shook hands Trollope suggested that she might be happier if she married a Christian. Perhaps she would, she said ; perhaps she'd be better with no husband at all ; " but I don't think I'll ever be happy no more. 'Tis so dull ; goodbye." She walked out of the room and he did not see her again ; but she remained in his mind, a lesser version of Maria in the Sentimental Journey. Though he could not, he added, ruefully, tell his story so well as Sterne.

As he saw more of the Jamaican countryside, Trollope's

attitude to the island softened. Riding from house to house with an attendant groom he was able to appreciate the landscape at leisure. The innumerable rivers tumbling from the hills delighted him, and the clusters of bamboo that shed a Gothic twilight on their banks. Then there were the silk-cotton trees, with their straight tall trunks and skirt-like buttresses, and it amused him to count upon his fingers the varieties of the parasite plants. Port Antonio was pleasant, and the village of Annotta Bay, and the great unbroken expanse of trembling sugar cane—some 4,000 acres—in the part of the island known as St. Georges in the East. Riding over Mount Diabolo he descended to St. Anne's, visiting the almost prosperous townships of Falmouth and Montego Bay. From a house on the border of the parishes of Hanover and Westmoreland he admired the cultivated, park-like panorama, and the beautifully cared-for properties, most splendid amongst them Lord Howard de Walden's estate of Shuttlestone. On the hill of Newcastle he found agreeable hosts and a society exclusively equestrian. Young and old, male and female all were indefatigable riders, for it was the only method of negotiating the perilous ravines and rocky tracks of the Blue Mountains.

The social life of Jamaica was monotonous. The day began at six, with coffee in one's bedroom. At eight the gentlemen set out to ride. At ten the company sat down to a heavy meat breakfast washed down by beer, brandy and rum. In the daytime the white ladies did not venture out of doors, but at night, after the evening meal, they would drift out upon the wide verandahs, to sip coffee and to chatter beneath the glittering stars. At nine they withdrew and went to bed. This regular and languid existence was broken, rather frequently, by someone giving a formal dance. Dancing, like riding, was a passion with Jamaicans. Dances began at ten, and might end at five in the morning. Jamaicans seemed as energetic as they were affable.

The nostalgia of English colonists, and even of English creoles, for their mother country gave Trollope something to think about. Like other visitors he began to contrast French

A Valley in the Blue Mountains, Jamaica

[*From Kingsley's " At Last,"* 1870

A Mangrove Swamp, Trinidad

[*From Kingsley's " At Last,"* 1870

The High Woods in Trinidad

and British colonial ideals. Like them too he suspected that
in some ways the French was a superior system. "The
Frenchman's object," he most truly observed, "is to carry his
Paris with him ; to make a Paris for himself, whether it be in
a sugar island among the Antilles or in a trading town upon
the Levant." One day in Martinique, or one conversation
with an educated French negro, will confirm this judgment.
At Basse-Terre in Guadaloupe we find a Breton fishing town
set down beside a jade-green tropical sea ; among the cane
fields and the villages of that island you come suddenly upon
a bust of Columbus or a statue of Victor Hugo upon a pedestal ;
everywhere, in the very lay-out of the country, is evidence of
the French spirit and the French taste. Why, Cashel had
often wondered, why if French culture can be exported cannot
we say the same of ours ?

Hospitable and friendly though Jamaicans were, Trollope
was appalled by their prejudices. They might with equal
reason have been appalled by his. One of his chief resent-
ments—bred perhaps by too long a sojourn in Ireland—was
against Roman Catholicism, particularly in its more exotic
forms. He despised the priests of Cuba, with their "doll of
a Madonna " decked in muslins and ribbons, and their efforts
to teach the negroes to sing hymns. Catholic churches
throughout the islands he dismissed shortly as "very ugly "
buildings : "we all know what is a large Roman Catholic
church, built in the worst taste and by a combination of the
lowest attributes of Gothic and Latin architecture." Like so
many aspects of the Victorian approach to the West Indies,
this anti-Catholic bias involved a paradox. English distaste
for the Catholicism of islands discovered by Columbus and
named by him and his compatriots in honour of the Trinity,
the apostles and the saints is a little incongruous. If Columbus
found a bay that seemed to him outstandingly beautiful he
called it Santa Gloria ; a new island with three hilltops against
the horizon was christened Trinidad. The English, ever
conscious of a more immediate and material Power, contented
themselves with naming their settlements after a Hanoverian
monarch or a Stuart queen.

From Jamaica Trollope went to Cuba, where he visited a sugar estate worked by slavery, and learned with disgust that " the Roman Catholic religion is alone allowed, and that is at its very lowest point." The sights of the capital, Havana, did little to justify its fame : of the three main buildings in the town the Opera House had been wrecked by an explosion of gas, the Cathedral was " devoid of beauty " and the palace of the Captain-General made only a " moderately imposing effect." The famous Paseo, a road running for half a mile outside the town wall, with seats and avenues of trees, might be unlike anything else in the West Indies, but no European would be able to understand why it was so eulogised. But there were picturesque touches even in this squalid and dis- appointing scene—the long volantes, those strange carriages swung forward on high wheels, that rocked along the Paseo of an evening, with their gaily dressed occupants sitting side by side. The volantes, he heard, were so valued by their owners that they were not consigned to a coach-house but kept in the dining-room or the hall ; they were driven by huge negroes in white breeches, scarlet jackets and high leather boots. The Cuban people he thought simple but superstitious. Their amusements—such as dancing to a military band in the plaza before the palace of an evening—were certainly innocuous. While Trollope was in Cuba American agitation for the cession of the island was just getting well under weigh. His own sympathies were divided ; the insolence of the American claim repelling him, while its likely effect upon the slave-trade inclined him in its favour. But he was too thoroughly English a character to look with any sympathy upon the firm if casual Spanish rule.

Steaming down the Windward Islands Trollope got glimpses of St. Kitts and Nevis, Antigua, Dominica, St. Lucia, St. Vincent and Grenada. The prosperity of the French islands, Guadaloupe and Martinique, astonished him as much as the poverty of the English towns of Castries and Roseau. But wherever he went there was something wrong ; and it was not till he reached British Guiana that he found a place entirely to his taste. Unfortunately when Trollope likes anything, he seems unable to avoid being facetious about it : " the men of Demerara are never angry and the women are never cross. Life flows along on a perpetual stream of love, smiles, champagne and small talk. Everybody has enough of everything. The form of Government is a mild despotism tempered by sugar." Really B. G. was too good to be true—the people were as healthy as they were happy, the treasury had a surplus, trade throve, there were no cabs in Georgetown because everyone who might have wanted them kept a private carriage.

Almost as wealthy as Demerara, but far less enticing, was Barbados, " a very respectable little island " though with few attractions for strangers. He did not, however, care much for Barbadians. The negroes were heavier, more broadly built, more insolent and more peevish than others he had seen. The white people were to all intents and purposes intolerable. They were purse-proud, they were self-glorious, short-tempered and extravagant. Even the negroes had luxurious habits, their women refusing to hold up their dresses as they walked for fear of being thought to grudge soiling a few yards of muslin petticoat. He longed to be " thrown among " the coloured Barbadians, but somehow they seemed both less numerous and less easy to meet than their counterparts in Jamaica. In fact it was as hard to talk with them here as it was to avoid doing so in Kingston.

Before leaving the West Indies for the " retrograding " civilisations of Central America, Trollope spent two days in Trinidad. The shores of the island seemed to him as beautiful as anything he had seen in the Caribbean, the trees along the steep northern coasts, the creeks that invited picnic parties— " with straw hats and crinoline, pigeon pies and champagne." Port of Spain was still building, and many of the streets were not yet lined with houses and shops. Government House itself was being reconstructed, and the Governor and his family were living in a large cottage in the Botanic Gardens. An outbreak of spotted fever at St. James' Barracks had caused the evacuation of the soldiers on to the Savannah, which was dotted with military tents. Typically, he explored the possibilities of organising black regiments and tried to assess the benefits of coolie immigration. In many ways Trollope was an ideal visitor for the West Indies ; he enjoyed examining and contrasting, asking questions and making notes ; and there can be few parts of the globe which present greater contrasts and more variety, problems more intricate or facts more bizarre than the islands of the British West Indies.

It was already March when Trollope was in Trinidad and he still had far to travel and much to do. He was in Costa Rica for Passion Week, watching the ceremonies with a sceptical interest, the great wax figures from Guatamala and the segregation of men and women in church. The Costa Ricans held no appeal for him. Their Spanish society was so formal. They never seemed to give parties at all. It was all so very different from the gay English life of Jamaica, the long drinks and the short drinks, the riding and the dancing, schottisches and galopades. But then however much he might profess a theoretical admiration for the results of French colonial rule, Trollope more than most other English travellers preferred an English culture and a way of life he understood.

When the last car door had slammed, and the last car had swept out towards the Savannah from Government House gates, Cashel returned alone to the empty ballroom to super-intend the switching off of the fans and the lights. One after another the chandeliers ceased to glitter, until the whole great room was in darkness, and the tall windows which had before let out the yellow bars of electric light now let in the strong pale beams of the moon. Cashel stood there a few moments before going to bed. He was thinking of Trollope's dances : then it had been the schottische and the galopade, now it was the Palais Glide and the Lambeth Walk : always an imitation of some aspect of English life that was in essence tawdry and trivial : little of English dignity or of English worth ? We could not expect, nor should we like, to find a Barchester in Guatamala. We might have liked, but we cannot now expect, to find one in Jamaica or in Trinidad.

Night Scene at Falmouth, Jamaica

[From a lithograph by J. B. Kidd

[From an engraving after an anonymous portrait

Robert Dudley

Chapter Three

THE YOUNG GENERAL

1595

And there, too, might be gold, and gems, and
all the wealth of Ind. Who knew ? Why not ?
Kingsley : *Westward Ho !*
chapter xvii

"You must try," said the archbishop, "to go and see Caracas."

"I know," Cashel answered, "I know." He knew too how thin was his chance of being allowed to cross the Gulf.

It was that moment of the evening—just after sunset—when the receding daylight seems to linger over the island, a blue mist that thickens while you watch it into night. They stood at the gate of the archbishop's bungalow, and Cashel was taking his leave after a close talk of several hours. The archbishop's white soutane gleamed against the darkening hibiscus hedge that cut off his piece of garden from the steep public lane. The strident colours of the hibiscus blossoms had been blotted out till morning. One of his grace's thin white hands, an amethyst ring on a finger, gripped the top of the garden-gate : his face too showed white beneath his skullcap, a bony classical face like the face on an ancient coin. Earlier in the evening Cashel had been noticing how worn the archbishop looked, with his exhausted eyes and his veined temples, but now the twilight had simplified the complex features into a narrow oval of whiteness set above the white oblong of his scapula. The archbishop had spent many decades as a priest in the British West Indies and he stood at his gate with infinite detachment smiling a precise smile. He knew, loved and utterly understood the islands, yet his heart yearned for the nearby continent with its solid monuments of Catholic culture and its inheritance from Portugal and Spain.

Quite suddenly the stillness was broken open by a shout of

singing that came up from the church at the bottom of the lane : negro voices at the Latin Benediction hymns. Stepping through the gate with an abrupt movement that seemed unsuitable but was in fact characteristic, the archbishop swung off down the lane. He turned to Cashel :

" Does it not do your heart good to hear it, my friend ? "

They parted at the Sacristy door.

As Cashel wandered back to Government House grounds, cutting across the corner of a public field in which a giant and melancholy tree had begun to drop its weighty fruit, he recapitulated in his mind all that he could remember of the evening's talk. The archbishop had spoken with suppressed enthusiasm of the South American continent, of the Spanish settlers, of the early Christian missions in this fetid western world ; of the architecture of the Venezuelan townships deploring by contrast how little there was left in Trinidad itself. The power and grandeur of Christianity had been his central theme, and he had spoken too, earnestly and by analogy with the laws of tropical nature, upon the human soul. Glancing at the hibiscus hedges he had warned Cashel against mere efflorescence, reminding him that flowers though beautiful were worthless without fruit. Sitting on a rocking-chair by the open door of the pinewood parlour, a plain black crucifix nailed to the wall above his head, Cashel had listened with silent attention as the archbishop applied the grid of Dominican theory to the soul. At first the attention had been also polite and sceptical, but gradually he realised how well it all seemed to fit, the very inflexibility being an advantage. Through the doorway he could see the garden in the heat of the late afternoon, the sun glaring on the verdant foliage, the profuse red blooms in the green hedge behind which bobbed the fantastic headgear of negro ladies shambling up and down the little lane. Outside in the sun all was madness and extravagance ; and in this cool small room an old man sat calmly applying a medieval theory to the human soul, to all souls, to the life of the island, of the continent and of the world. Was it just the contrast that made it sound so tempting ? Cashel had reached the end of his walk. Looking at the

fretted window-frames of the cottage he confessed to himself
that he could not, and perhaps never would, make up his mind
about such things. An agnostic who had never considered
his theological position, he felt that Christianity was impossible
to accept ; and yet judged by its works out here, how true.

In a bookrack in the living-room of the cottage were wedged
a number of books that he had borrowed from the archbishop
and could not yet make up his mind to return. They were
journals, records and diaries of English travellers in the
Caribbean : journals of visitors separated from each other,
some by occupation or outlook or temperament, others merely
by the fact of Time. Amongst these books were Froude's
English in the West Indies in olive linen ; Dudley's *Voyage* in
the bright blue cloth of the Hakluyt Society ; Lady Nugent's
Journal, a fat black volume with stout gilt letters down its
spine ; Henry Coleridge's *Six Months in the West Indies* in
white linen, and next to it Mrs. Carmichael's spirited
defence of Slavery in the same coloured binding ; Gurney's
Winter in the West Indies (a tedious book) ; a bound pamphlet
of a naval surgeon's adventures in Marie Galante ; and
several more. Cashel was working his way through them, and
some of them he had read two or three times. As a solid
background he kept Edwardes' *History* of the islands, two
quarto volumes with red labels and stamped with gold laurel
wreaths, on his desk ; but this, to tell the truth, he seldom
read.

At the moment he was still busy with the Elizabethans, and
selecting Dudley from the bookshelf he now switched on a
lamp and lay down on a couch by one of the windows. It had
got quite dark outside in the garden, and the moon was not yet
up. The long room of the cottage was dark too, save for the
bright coin of electric light about the couch. Lying in the
light Cashel looked unnaturally vivid, with his white cotton
suit and his sky-blue book. The couch itself was nondescript
and low with squat, elaborate feet : the window-frame above
reflected the lamplight in its lower panes, but its general outline was dim ; the trunk of the Saman tree beyond it was
hardly visible at all.

There was silence throughout the Botanic Garden, and silence lay over the lawns of Government House. The Union Jack had been hauled down from its flagpole. The frogs had not yet begun to croak. Cashel lay very still, absorbed in Dudley's narrative. Occasionally a big flying ant would whir through the circle of light, to rattle against the bulb of the lamp.

In 1595 Robert Dudley was a handsome and no doubt an elegant young man, tall, compact, with red hair and large bulging almond-shaped eyes. The bastard of the great Earl of Leicester, Elizabeth's favourite, and of Douglas Lady Sheffield, he had been brought up in some seclusion on the tranquil Sussex sea-coast at Offington by Worthing. In the year of the Armada, the year also of his father's death, he had gone up to Oxford. In due time he reached the court, in every way a good example of the final generation that was sprouting up about the old Queen. Elizabeth herself was now spangled, bewigged, gaudy and spattered with jewels, even more incisive, more terrifying ; but the obsequious young men who genuflected when she spoke to them knew quite well that theirs was a future she could not control. Her glory had become an evening glory, and recognising it they must have seen that their careers lay before them like elongated shadows, projected into the new century, across the next reign. Among his contemporaries Robert Dudley was already noted for his knowledge of physics and chemistry, his mathematic learning, and his passion for navigation and the sea. He was also, according to Anthony à Wood, the " first of all that taught a dog to sit in order to catch partridges." He wrote a fine looped hand ; he wore the fashionable ear-jewels ; the clustering locks of his auburn hair reached to the nape of his neck. His gallantry, which was of that cool but showy variety that his contemporaries loved, was never questioned. His brain was active and enquiring and in 1594 he decided that the time had come to equip an expedition and set sail for the South Sea. His motives are easy to analyse. Like Raleigh's, on a different journey they were :

" To seek new worlds, for gold, for praise, for glory," though unlike him Dudley had never been an intimate royal favourite, and was never impelled to voyage by disgrace. Nor had he to feign extremes of disappointed love for the old Queen :

> To seek new worlds, for gold for praise for glory,
> To try desire, to try love severed far,
> When I was gone she sent her memory
> More strong than were ten thousand ships of war,

> To call me back, to leave great honour's thought,
> To leave my friends, my fortune, my attempt,
> To leave the purpose I so long had sought,
> And hold both cares and comforts in contempt.

Raleigh wrote twelve books of such verses in his *Book of the Ocean to Cynthia*, to reinstate himself in the Queen's favour. Yet though no disgrace was in question, Elizabeth did suddenly and inexplicably clamp the royal veto down on Dudley's proposed voyage. It was typical of her methods that he was allowed to perfect his preparations before being forbidden to sail. He was horribly disappointed. It had cost him a great deal of money and it was an expedition that promised adventure and renown. But he could not move while the Queen's ban remained, and so he found himself in his own words " constrained . . . to prepare another course for the West Indies, without hope there to do anything worth note." " So common is it indeed," he wrote in deprecation to Hakluyt, ". . . as it is not worth the registering." It is easy to see what he meant. The exploits of Hawkins and Drake on the Spanish Main in the 'seventies, already far away, had blunted the edge of the adventure, those thrilling midnight attacks on Nombre de Dios, the silent ambushing of the mule-trains from Panama. There was nothing really new to be done on the Main, and Dudley who was acutely ambitious aimed at novelty. It was with boredom, or so he afterwards affected, that he eventually weighed anchor in Southampton Roads on November 6th, 1594.

The fleet at first consisted of an admiral, the *Bear*, a ship of two hundred tons, in which Dudley sailed, the *Bear's Whelp*, under Captain Munck, and two pinnaces facetiously called the *Frisking* and the *Earwig*. The names of English ships at this time suggest admirably the prevalent spirit : the *Moon-shine*, the *Garland*, the *Angel*, the *Ark Raleigh*, and, more sinister and strange, Lord Cumberland's famous ship, the *Malice Scourge*. There were many theories on the naming of ships. Sir Richard Hawkins in his *Observations*, printed in 1622, gives some. Never, he implores his readers, give to " terrestrial works " names merely representative of " celestial character." He exemplifies his plea by calling attention to the awful fates of *The Revenge* and *The Thunderbolt*. Sombre names should always be avoided. He describes the unwisdom of his stepmother Lady Hawkins (" no prophetess, though religious and most virtuous . . . and of a very good under-standing ") who when asked to launch a new ship built in the Thames in 1588 had called it the *Repentance*. To her step-son's shocked remonstrances this lady bleakly answered that " Repentance was the safest ship we could sail in to purchase the haven of heaven." Such medieval sentiments were almost painfully out of date. But in fact so far as the *Repentance* was concerned it did not matter, for coming up the river from Deptford the ship was noticed by the Queen, proceeding to Greenwich in her barge. She ordered the bargemen to row round the ship, and " viewing her from post to stern " declared she disliked nothing but the name, insisting that that be changed. The *Dainty* was the alternative she chose.

Cashel had once read through Hawkins' *Observations*. From it he had gained a romantic but fanciful picture of life aboard a Tudor ship. He had read of methods for avoiding scurvy (one of the best being to make the men dance) ; of the necessity of celebrating Sunday properly ; of the importance of shutting cabin windows against the dangerous light of the African moon ; of how to extract civett from wild-cats ; of what cocoa-nuts look like and where to find ambergreece ; of how to hunt the penguin and how to sheath ships' sides ; of wine on a ship as more dangerous than an enemy. These were the trivia that had stayed in his mind, mingling with

St. Joseph and the Caroni River, Trinidad

Cedar Point, Mount Tamana, Trinidad : looking out towards the Gulf of Paria

scraps of Tudor verse, Spenserian affectations about sea-travel :

> . . . . the sea that is
> A world of waters heaped up on high,
> Horrible, hideous, roaring with hoarse cry.

And alternatively :

> " These be the hills," quoth he, " the surges high
> On which fair Cynthia her herds doth feed ;
> Her herds be thousand fishes with their fry,
> Which in the bosom of the billows breed.
> Of them the shepherd which hath charge in chief
> Is Triton blowing loud his wreathed horn,
> At sound whereof they all for their relief
> Wend to and fro at evening and at morn."

Robert Dudley, who in old age had a European reputation as a maritime authority, had a more prosaic attitude to the sea. Yet after all this was a first voyage as well as a first visit to the Tropics, and his behaviour in Trinidad was not altogether lacking in romanticism.

Dudley reached Trinidad on January 31st, 1595, a Saturday, after a stormy journey by way of Cape Blanco and the Canaries. It was early in the morning that they sighted land " which was the main continent between Brazil and India, and within some two hours after, our good General himself descried the island of Trinidado, for which we had always born." After a day passed in gazing on the steep and gentle outlines of the island, then yet more thickly wooded than to-day, they anchored in a bay which Dudley named Bay Pelican " for the great abundance of Pelicans that we see there." They settled down to plan the exploration of Trinidad.

Dudley was not quite the first Englishman and by no means the first European to examine Trinidad. The Edward Bonaventure, returning home in 1593 after rounding the Cape of Good Hope and visiting St. Helena, had stopped at the island for refreshing, and Jacob Whiddon, who had been sent out there by Raleigh to report on the possibilities of a Guiana expedition, had also been to Trinidad. To the Spaniards still intent on penetrating Eldorado, Trinidad became an

3

administrative problem. Fifty miles long, some thirty-five
wide, lying at the north-eastern tip of the South American
continent, Trinidad had been found by Columbus in 1498, in
the course of his third voyage of discovery. He had sailed
with his main fleet of six ships from San Lucar at the end of
May, and passing by Madeira and the Canaries (whence he
despatched three vessels direct to his settlement of Hispaniola)
he had continued on into the still heat of the South Western
Atlantic. For eight days they had experienced burning
weather, and then a favourable wind sprang up and blew them
further and yet further westwards through a summer sea. As
July ended water and food began to fail. Columbus decided
to turn north, back to Hispaniola. Then on July 31st a sailor
saw land from the round-top, fifteen leagues to the west, a dark
shape on the horizon with three mountains jutting up. The
island, which they reached at evening, seemed to Columbus as
fresh and green as the gardens of Valencia in March. They
rounded a cape, which proved to have a harbour but no satisfactory anchorage, and though they saw huts and natives there,
they did not land but continued five leagues along the coast
towards the west. At another cape, which he named Punta
del Arenal, Columbus disembarked some of his men, to rest
and to collect water and wood. There was no one about.
The ground was trampled thickly by the feet of animals, but
none were to be seen ; only a dead and hornless species of
goat, which they recognised as a catamountain. It is a strange
arresting picture : the ships anchored in the calm still sea, the
water lapping, the low shores of the island, and the steep
wooded hills behind; the silence broken only by bird cries; all
the time the knowledge that somewhere in the forests there
were eyes watching, but no one to be seen. On the next day
a canoe came from eastwards carrying twenty-five young men
armed with bows and arrows, and with bucklers of wood.
They were, noted Columbus, of fine physical proportions,
whiter than other Indians he had seen, very graceful, even
handsome, with their hair worn long and straight in the
Spanish way. Round their heads embroidered scarves were
folded, and some of them wore scarves about their bodies too.

They spoke to Columbus' sailors, but in an unknown tongue. For two hours the Spaniards tried to coax them to come nearer. Each time they tried, the Indians apprehensively withdrew. No interest was shown in a series of brass basins and mirrors flashed alluringly in the tropical sunlight. Soon Columbus had what proved to be a most unfortunate idea. Ordering drums to be beaten, and pipes and tabors to be played, he told a troop of his younger sailors to dance upon the decks. The effect of this supreme attempt to fascinate the natives was immediate and quite unexpected. At the first notes of the thin music, and the first movements of the figures on the deck, the Caribs drew their bows and sent a flight of arrows in amongst the dancers. The sailors replied with a discharge from their crossbows, which drove the Indians to refuge under the poop of another of the ships. Here they seem to have talked to the crew, and accepted presents from them, and were permitted to go peacefully away to the shore. They promised to take the captain of the vessel on shore with them, but while he was asking Columbus' sanction they rowed quickly off in their canoe. They were never seen by the sailors again. It was not an auspicious beginning for European influence in Trinidad.

Three decades after this abortive visit, a Governor and Alguazil Mayor was appointed for the island of Trinidad. This was Antonio Sedeno, Contador of the Island of San Juan. His appointment was confirmed in Madrid in July of 1530, the warrant being signed in Charles V's absence by Isabella, the paragon Castilian Empress, whose serene beauty has been made familiar to later generations by Titian's posthumous portrait. The preamble to this warrant speaks in conventional terms of Sedeno's zeal for the service of God and the imperial realms in offering to build a fort upon Trinidad, and to instal a priest there to baptise the Indians. Sedeno was not very successful, for four years later an effort to find him on the island failed, and only his tapia fort, its earth ramparts falling away, thirty-five sick Spaniards inside it, was left to mark his passage.

Spanish relations with the Caribs on the Main were anyway

uneven and difficult. In spite of a series of royal cedulas, the Europeans continued to treat the Indians with great severity, destroying the early friendliness and first confidence of many of the tribes. The Indians, cannibals among them, did not hesitate to retaliate. They massacred Spanish priests and civilians, and displayed the heads on pikes. But although the general tone was one of torpor, there was an outlandish, a staccato vitality about the Spanish Empire. The bitterness of quarrels between the Spaniards themselves was only equalled by the fierceness of their hatred for the Indians. The climate was then no more conducive to geniality among those fresh from Europe than it is to-day. And the Spaniards found it nearly impossible to get the Indians to work properly in the mines. An ominous note is struck in June 1532 when de Castro suggests to the King of Spain that negroes are required to exploit the gold found in the hills. Here are the seeds of the Slave Trade, and of many centuries of West Indian miseries.

Often as the car spun out along the Eastern Road from Port of Spain, through the straggling, stinking Indian hamlet of Toonapoona, to St. Joseph and the plantations of the Government Farm, Cashel tried to imagine what sort of an island it was that Dudley, and after him Raleigh, had found. St. Joseph is now a residential district for Port of Spain ; it covers the site of the tapia huts and little houses, with the big church and the Franciscan monastery in their centre, which Walter Raleigh burned in almost biblical revenge. St. Joseph was founded in 1592. After Sedeno's failure to subdue it, it seems that the island of Trinidad was left to lie fallow, and the Indians, the parrots and the catamountains permitted to continue untroubled their noisy existence on the Savannahs and in the High Woods. But in May 1592 Domingo de Vera was ordered by Berrio (to whom the island had this time been entrusted by the King) to build a town on Trinidad. The town was to be called San Josef de Oruna. Berrio said that he had already lost a hundred pesos of gold in his search for Eldorado, and in his last expedition up the Orinoco he had lost too eighty men. He appealed to royal piety ; the light of

River Scene, Trinidad

Forest Scene, Trinidad

Bamboo Arches near Port of Spain, Trinidad

[From a lithograph by Ciceri

Faith must be brought to the Trinidad Caribs. Incidentally, he added, the settlement would obstruct English and French pirates who were using the island to refit their ships. It would also prevent the kidnapping of Caribs for the slave-markets of Margarita, stop the natives of Dominica, Granada and Matalino from attacking the island, and thus save the Trinidad Indians from being eaten by cannibals.

When de Vera, Berrio's *maestro de campo*, had landed his men and munitions in Trinidad he chose a site for the new town, close to the Caroni river, and between the green hills and the sea. Sweeping his sword around him he cut down the wild plants, declaring the island taken in the King's name. A wooden cross had been constructed, forty foot high, and with the help of his Franciscan chaplain, de Vera jammed this into the ground. The cross stood there in the clearing made by the sword-blade, heavy swathes of tangled foliage withering about it. As de Vera proclaimed that he would guard the island against all comers, the soldiers yelled and yelled again: " *Biba el Rey.*" After marking out the site for the church, Nuestra Santa Fe de la Concepcion, of a house for the Governor and a prison building, de Vera prohibited the enslavement of any Indian on the island, and announced that the penalty for giving them arms was death.

The Caroni river, up which pirogues were able to make their way, flows still beside the site of old San Josef. To Cashel it was absurdly reminiscent of a Constable landscape : it flowed between low lush meadows of fresh grass. On one of its banks now grows a huge grove of cultivated bamboo, with roadways through it, and an olive twilight everywhere. Nightjars with crimson eyes, like the eyes of witches, flutter and flop their clumsy wings within the depths of this dim wood. Walking along the shadowy paths, Cashel would come suddenly upon a bend of the Caroni river, vivid fields upon its further bank, a scene framed for you by the curves of the lithe bamboos.

On February 2nd, 1596, three days after he had anchored in Pelican Bay the Indians (bolder than their forbears of 1490)

swarmed on board Dudley's ships. They brought with them
tobacco, nuts and fruit ; but no gold and no pearls. In
exchange they snatched knives, bugles, beads, hatchets and
and fishing hooks. If it was gold the strangers were after,
these Indians said they knew of a mine not far away along the
coast. Dudley organised a squad of men to go there, under
the command of one of his captains. After eighty miles of
toiling the men came upon the gold-mine. It turned out to
be a mine of marcasite. This mattered little to Dudley : for
on the following day he got his men together and marched
with them " through the deep sands and in a most extreme hot
day " to the interior of the island. Reaching the marcasite
mine they loaded themselves till midnight with this worthless
ore. A mist was gathering between the tree trunks, and
Dudley, " unaccustomed, God he knows, to walk on foot,"
was exhausted. He ordered boughs and branches to be
lopped from the prolific trees, and spread for him upon the
soft ground. Lying down on them he slept. Over the still
body an ensign, Barrow, held his master's colours. Dudley's
men solemnly ringed the sleeper about. Like the peevish
lovers of the wood of Athens, the young man lay there under
the vast exotic trees. His sleep was soon disturbed. Fireflies, which usually enraptured every visitor to the tropics,
were regarded with suspicion by Dudley's inexperienced men.
As they flashed in the depths of the forest the flies looked
" like so many light matches " to the guard, who frightened by
the noiseless sparkle shouted and gave the alarm. When
dawn broke the expedition went back to the ships. They
marched pompously to the sound of drum and trumpet, much
of the way through the sea water, waist deep—" an unusual
thing for (Dudley) being a courtier but not unfit . . . being our
General in India." Dudley had wisely avoided contact with
the Spanish settlers at San Josef. He knew that the town,
though poverty-stricken was strong, and he prudently ignored
the Spanish owners of the island in taking formal possession of
it in the Queen's name. For this ceremony a plate of lead was
engraved with a wordy Latin inscription : describing how
Dudley, the Earl of Leicester's son, had landed on the island

with his forces. When finished this plate was draped in silver lace and carried in procession to a hilltop near the marcasite mine. Here, while the general's colours were displayed and the bugles blown, it was nailed to a tree. The progress up the hill had been accompanied by the shrilling of trumpets and the rumble of drums. Captain Wyatt who held the plate stepped out and read the inscription aloud in a firm voice. He kissed the royal arms. He fixed the plate to the tree and made a short oration. Once again the martial music echoed and re-echoed on the spungy forest air, and the shouts of the soldiers crying God Save the Queen.

Dudley had made a tentative arrangement with Walter Raleigh to meet him at the Orinoco delta. It was, then, to that river's many mouths that his ships set sail on leaving Pelican Bay. There he waited for Raleigh ; unaware that Raleigh's ships had reached Trinidad just a week after he had himself left. As Raleigh did not put in an appearance at the Orinoco Dudley pursued his way onwards in the middle of March. He was bent on finding the vessels of the Silver Fleet then on its way to Spain. He did not come across these ships but he did meet " foul weather enough to scatter many fleets." Leaving the course he had set towards the Bermudas he returned towards Europe by the Azores. One May morning of this homeward voyage they sighted a big Spanish man-of-war—" upright as a church." Pursuing her, they left her in a sinking condition after a running fight of forty-eight hours. It was a stimulating fight for the English, whose spirits had perhaps begun to flag after the marcasite fiasco and the missing of Raleigh. As the sulphur spluttered and the smoke whirled away on the wind, Dudley's staff was shot from his very hand. The cannon balls came lumbering at the ships' sides plunging, hissing, into the dark blue sea. At the height of the battle one of Dudley's captains brought him a page to be recommended for his courage. This youth had smashed his firing piece. Jobson stood in the General's cabin while the battle raged outside, urbanely quoting the popular lines from the *Spanish Tragedy* :

This is my son, gracious General,
Of whom though from his tender infancy,
My loving thoughts did never hope but well,
He never pleased his father's eyes till now,
Nor filled my heart with overcloying joy,
Long may he live to serve my General.

Dudley was delighted, and thanking Jobson for the "fine conceit and fine application" and the boy for his daring he presented the latter with a firing-piece of his own.

After a voyage of six months, Robert Dudley landed at St. Ives and rode to London. He broke his journey at Wilton House. For all his affected boredom the voyage must have changed him considerably ; at any rate it had not changed Trinidad, for it needed more than a couple of trumpets and a leaden coat of arms to civilise those wild resisting hills. What can we know of Dudley's reactions ? He had crossed the South Atlantic under the stars ; as the air became slowly cooler and the impregnable grandeur of the island forests a memory merely, as the sunsets grew less fantastic and the Southern Cross faded away, what marks were left by his experience upon the surface of that arrogant mind ? With what tales did he regale the precious and melancholy Countess of Pembroke at Wilton ? What strong colours did he bring back with him to incarnadine her pale Arcadian world ?

There was a short step, and a noise of clanking on the gravel outside the cottage. Cashel closed his book. The figure that edged into the room might have that moment folded a gold-fringed parasol and stepped down from a Genoese Van Dyck : it was in fact the youngest negro footman, wearing a waistcoat of canary-stripe, and carrying a can of boiling water for the bath in either hand.

Chapter Four

THE POET'S NEPHEWS

1825

A nigger fore and aft,
A nigger on the shaft
And a pair of island Arabs to draw us on in state.
Barbuda rhyme

CASHEL SOON LEARNED that Government House, constructed
in the 'seventies, did not occupy the site of any earlier building.
The house of the first English Governors of Trinidad had
stood up on an eminence and not, like its successor, in a
bottom. Damaged by earthquake in 1826, the Residence at
St. Anne's had been ultimately abandoned, and its ruins, sodden
by a century of tropical rains, and shrouded by a rich growth
of tropical weeds, have been practically obliterated. You can
see the hill on which it had been set from the dining-room
windows of the present Government House. Cashel had
found that there were two ways of reaching the site. One,
across the modern lawns, the hard tennis-courts, a narrow lane,
a rough field and, finally, the high road, took you scrambling
up a path along the hillside, and brought you at length breath-
less to the summit. The other, which involved walking out
on to the road round the Savannah, and along another road
that forked left from it, and then plunging sharply off behind
a police station, took you into the old carriage drive, which
still sweeps nobly up the hill beneath silk-cotton trees. Which-
ever way you went (and the carriage drive was unquestionably
the most agreeable) you came out into a small, level wood.
Only the curious flatness of the ground, and occasional bricks
and stumpy pieces of wall-foundations hidden in the undergrowth showed that a building had stood here. Otherwise
all was neglect. Where once had risen the white, plain,
dignified Residence in which Sir Ralph Woodford had
urbanely entertained his guests, there was now a wilderness.

At your feet strange grasses nodded their feathery heads, and lithe unhealthy roots clutched at each other (and at you) : fantastic trees tilted their spiky branches above you : and, all around the quivering shrubs, veridian leaves, wild thorns and poisonous berries formed a cage of living greenery. If you braved these, and slashing down the foliage peered out from the hilltop, you got a clear idea of what could be seen from the windows of Old Government House : " the town, the church and the gulph lie in sight, and within a mile is the entrance of the famous valley of Maraval, and still farther on the coast the less celebrated but hardly less beautiful vale of Diego Martin." Sometimes Cashel did this, lingering on his way down again to look at the great grey tree-trunks beside the carriage-way.

On a certain March morning in the year 1825, four horses harnessed to a smart open landau trotted down the drive from Old Government House. They were followed by a single horse drawing a gig. As this equipage passed briskly down the curving carriage-way the early sunlight, penetrating the canopy of trees, flickered on the door-panels of the landau and on their painted coats-of-arms. The landau, closely followed by the gig, clattered out into the road. The party in these vehicles comprised the Governor, Sir Ralph Woodford ; the new bishop of Barbados, Dr. Coleridge ; the bishop's cousin, Mr. Henry Coleridge ; the bishop's two chaplains ; and a gentleman who was named Sainthill. The immediate object of the sortie (one of a series designed to show his lordship the island) was the cacao plantation of La Pastora, owned by a Spanish planter and situated some miles from Port of Spain. At the outskirts of that city the carriages halted for a moment, at a crystal spring which gushed down into a stone basin, where, shaded by evergreens, the negro girls of the city bathed their feet. After admiring this scene, and hearing from Sir Ralph that the spring was jocularly called (by the English) the Governor's grog shop, they resumed their journey : bowling down the dry roads and lanes until they saw rising at last in the distance the tall straight trees of La Pastora, trees which served as shelter to the delicate cacao plants. As they approached they could discern between the tree-trunks, the wild and flaming beauty of the red Bois Immortel. The plantation was situated in a romantic natural amphitheatre in the woods: the house and estate works lay at the edge of the trees. The visitors were shown the cool, shadowy passage-ways between the trees in which the cacao was reared, and found the central ride, with trim paths diverging from it in all directions, a delicious retreat after their dusty drive. Then, too, they met, to Mr. Henry Coleridge's great delight, the Spanish planter's three daughters, Dolores, Lorenza and Soledad.

As the title of his book indicated, Henry Nelson Coleridge spent *Six Months in the West Indies*. This facetious and rather detestable young man was the nephew, and later the son-in-law and the literary executor of the poet. Suffering in London from an unspecified rheumatic ailment, he had taken the opportunity of his cousin's appointment as first Bishop of Barbados and the Leeward Islands to try whether a change of climate could not effect what London doctors had failed to do. The bishop, William Hart Coleridge, was despatched to his scattered diocese in a British man-of-war in 1825 ; and after a few weeks in Barbados he set out in the sloop *Eden* on a thorough inspection of the Leeward Islands. Travelling with the bishop as his secretary, Henry Coleridge saw Dominica, Trinidad, St. Vincent, St. Lucia, Antigua and Monserrat at much closer quarters than most casual visitors manage to do. The state of Protestant Christianity in these Crown Colonies was not at that time satisfactory, and in the last years before the Abolition of slavery the English hierarchy had become suddenly anxious over the condition of negro souls. In Trinidad, that old Spanish possession, this anxiety was merely increased by the persistence of its Christian inhabitants in sticking to the Romish faith. Of all the things they saw during their six months' visitation, few exasperated Henry Coleridge so much as a French Catholic girl of Trinidad who giggled openly while the Bishop was conducting a Protestant marriage service for a number of negro couples in the settle-ment at Savannah Grande. It was not only with the " bestial

manners " and immodest dress of the slave population that the
Anglican missionaries had to contend.   Towards the close of
the Bishop's tenure of office, however, the Reformed Church
was flourishing in the Caribbees—by 1835 there were ninety-
nine clergy, forty-two schoolhouses, more than fifty parish
churches : a notable increase in quantity due to the earnest
labours of this sincere and able man.

The life of Henry Nelson Coleridge was short.   Born in
1797, the year of the Battle of the Nile, he died in 1843,
leaving to his widow Sara the completion of their joint task—
the editing of Samuel Taylor Coleridge's works.   Unlike his
cousin the bishop, who was plump and self-confident, with a
round but noble face and heavy-lidded eyes, Henry Coleridge
was sprightly, vivacious and sparkling.   He was considered
the cleverest and the most captivating of the younger Coleridge
generation : a poet, a diligent and erudite scholar, a Fellow of
Kings, he was also admired as a first-class wit : and this last
quality was his undoing.   He let no occasion for a joke slip
by : and everyone and everything he saw in the West Indies—
Spanish beauties, Creole girls, negro slaves, edible toads—
became automatically a subject for his facile humour.   Even
the tropical birds were not exempt :

> Hush-a-bye cornbird, on the tree top,
> When the wind blows thy cradle will rock ;
> If the bough breaks thy cradle will fall,
> Then down will come cradle, cornbird and all.

The " infantile silliness," " impertinence " and " coxcombry "
of certain passages of *Six Months in the West Indies* irritated
Samuel Taylor Coleridge ; especially as the book seemed to
him to be generally an instructive and amusing one.   Its chief
fault, the uncle wrote to another nephew, lay in its imitation of
Southey :   " the frequent obtrusion of offensive images—
sweating, etc.," constant and jocular references to food,
levities on the Odd and even on the Grotesque, all of which, in
short, could only be summed up by the synthetic noun
" Southeianism."   Oddly enough, Southey himself thought
the book a trifle foolish, and the style " yeasty ; " though " he

Town of Roseau, Dominica

The Pitons of St. Lucia, 1837

Holy Trinity Cathedral, Port of Spain, soon after its completion

Roman Catholic Cathedral, Port of Spain, built 1816–1832

saddens into excellent sense before the end." There was
another reason for Samuel Taylor Coleridge's vague disapproval. Throughout the book strange and tiresome references recur to a certain Eugenia, with whom the author makes
it clear that he is in love. One of these references—in which
the unknown lady is described as " my sister ere my wife "—
aroused the poet's suspicions : could his own daughter Sara
be the girl ? Enquiry revealed that she was without doubt
Eugenia : and that, in virtue of the secret exchange of a coral
ring for a lock of hair one day at Highgate, they regarded
themselves as betrothed. Quite apart from his annoyance at
his daughter's wish to " change her maiden state without
changing her maiden name," the poet declared that the
" mingling of romance in a book of facts, and of very important
ones, too, was not pleasant to my feelings." But he came
round to liking Henry in the end ; though he never showed
much affection for the bishop (" your episcopal cousin "), who
had seemed to him as a youth marked out for a literary career
and had obstinately chosen a missionary one.

At the time of the Coleridges' visit (twenty-eight years after
the British had captured Trinidad), Port of Spain promised to
be the finest town in the West Indies. It had been burned out
in a single conflagration in 1808, and the rigorous planning laws
passed after this catastrophe were still methodically enforced.
No house might be built of wood ; each block erected must
conform to a set pattern. Under the sane guidance of
Sir Ralph Woodford (Governor from 1813 until his death in
1828) a neat new English town was rising on the ashes of the
shoddy Latin port. French girls still chattered their patois in
the market place ; stumpy Spanish forts still stood out in
silhouette upon the hillsides ; but the names of the recon-
stituted streets were indicative of change that had taken place
in the island. The Rue des Trois Chandels had become
Duncan Street ; Laplace, George Street ; the Rue d'Herrara,
Henry Street. The sea had been pushed back from the lower
town by a breakwater and King Street set out on the recovered
land. Most symbolic of all an Anglican Cathedral, " one of
the most splendid and elegant things in the empire," now

pointed its trim tower towards the glittering night sky. The cathedral had an elliptical roof ; polished wainscoting ; an altar, an organ and a staircase all " in a corresponding style of richness and propriety," and was dedicated to the Holy Trinity.

The bishop's first journey, in April, took them from Barbados to Trinidad, St. Vincent and St. Lucia. In May they set out from Bridgetown again (always on board the sloop *Eden*) to visit Martinique, Dominica, Monserrat, Nevis, St. Kitts, Anguilla, Antigua and the marshy little islet of Barbuda. Everywhere they went they inspected churches : everywhere they were disappointed. The church at Roseau in Dominica, though well situated, was panelled in unpainted pitch pine, and the delicate Henry found himself " oppressed . . . in a remarkable manner " by the smell. Roseau boasted 2,000 Protestants against 16,000 Papists ; but of the hundred coloured persons who attended the bishop's morning service few carried prayer-books, fewer still seemed in any way acquainted with the ordinary Anglican ritual, and all had clearly come to stare at Dr. Coleridge sweating in his bands. In St. Vincent, where there were two churches in the whole island, the Methodists seemed to flourish like the green bay tree. Monserrat was largely under the influence of the tall, wicked Abbé O'Hannam, an Irish priest who confirmed the cousins' worst suspicions by gallantly toasting the Protestant bishop of Jamaica at dinner. Here there were two anglican churches : one, half a mile from the town, was literally kept together by the " manual skill " of the good rector, Mr. Luckock ; the other, St. Peters, had been out of commission for a year. At Nevis the exasperated bishop found five little churches, with truly delightful views to be got from over their churchyard walls. The Lowland church commanded the blue narrows, and the distant shores of St. Kitts ; Figtree Church in Lady Nelson's home parish, was perched halfway up a mountain overlooking the sea ; from the graveyard at Ginger-land you could spy Monserrat and Antigua ; the town church of the capital, Charlestown, was hedged in by evergreen bushes, and its burial ground was happily free from the pretentious mausoleums which, in the other islands, had

offended Henry Coleridge's purist taste. Also in Nevis were
two large and splendid private chapels, one built by Mr. Cottle,
the other by Mr. Huggins. The Nevis clergy, however, were
paid in kind—bad sugar : and that, with all its commercial
complications, the bishop refused to tolerate. At St. Kitts the
nine churches that lay in the shadow of bleak Mount Misery
were of uneven quality. That in Basseterre itself was badly
built, and now cheek by jowl with a Conventicle ; yet in its
rector Mr. Davis, the parish possessed one of the boldest native
preachers of the diocese. Anguilla quite simply had no
church at all. Antigua had one that almost rivalled Sir Ralph
Woodford's cathedral in Port of Spain.

Cashel sometimes wondered whether the bland and portly
young bishop had returned to Bridgetown very much dis-
couraged by his second journey in the *Eden*. It was a ram-
shackle diocese that he had been sent out to rule ; and the
prospect might well have filled with dismay a cleric chiefly
noted for the lovely intonations with which he read the
baptismal service at St. Andrews, Holborn. It was all so
painfully different from Ottery St. Mary, the precincts of St.
Pauls, or Kings Parade. Henry, it is true, did try to see a
similarity between a mountain ride to a Soufrière in Monserrat
and a ramble down the Devonshire lanes in which he and his
cousin had been reared. There were, of course, no primroses
and no violets ; instead of these " the snowy amaryllis drooped
her long petals " and the scarlet-crowned hibiscus bobbed in
the pale hedges of lime and orange-tree. The path ended
suddenly in a mysterious natural clearing or savannah, from
which Henry could see Guadaloupe, Redonda shining like an
emerald in the waves, and the majestic pyramid of Nevis
amidst slowly whirling vapours. It was not, after all, so very
like Devon, and the wind that fluttered his open shirt was hot
and moist. The bishop, who never accompanied his secretary
on these harum-scarum expeditions into the interior of
the islands, was meanwhile busy with Luckock the rector.
A catechist was needed to instruct some of the six thousand
unlettered slaves of Monserrat. After their visit, the
Coleridges felt sure that " means will not be wanting for still

further increasing the number and influence of those by whose
exertions a religious and moral spirit may be excited in the
slaves, and the peaceable subordination of the whole class
insured." Owing perhaps to the predominance of priests like
the Abbé O'Hannam the negro slaves of Monserrat talked
with an Irish brogue. But every day the Coleridge cousins
were discovering how slight a resemblance West Indian
accents and manners, houses and churches bore to their
British prototypes : or indeed to anything that two cultured
English gentlemen had ever experienced in all their lives
before.

Henry Coleridge's exuberance did not prevent his using to
the full that gift of the gods, the power to discriminate.
Where most West Indian visitors merely distinguished one
island from the next by its relative discomforts, he perceived
the essential differences in atmosphere which each landscape
creates. Trinidad he found Spanish American : Grenada
with its lagoon was " perfect Italy." The countryside of
Monserrat, though of a bold and rugged character, seemed
" unfinished." At St. Kitts the canefields were like green
velvet, and the vale of Basseterre seemed more gentle and rich
in contrast with the black peak of Mount Misery jutting above
it into an unclouded sky. The mountain-points of St. Lucia
were sharper, more " arrowy ; " the famous Pitons reminded
him of Coventry spires. In Dominica the trembling fern
forests in the recesses of the hills around Roseau excited him
most. Roseau had, at the time of his visit, hardly yet recovered from the effects of a fire that had burned it down one
Easter Sunday evening in 1781, nearly forty-five years before.
Behind the shuttered house-fronts the houses were empty
shells ; grass tufted the main street ; and native women sat at
work in the roadway beneath a tamarind or a mangrove's
shade. " All," he concluded, " is silent, and soft and lifeless
like a city in the Arabian nights, . . . stricken with enchant-
ment." Antigua was in the grand old colonial English style :
stately mansions with English parks and lawns about them,
and occupied by the hereditary planter families—Cedar Hill,
approached through a long avenue of white cedar-trees :

Betty's Hope with its pillared gateway ; the impressive estate of Green Castle. The flower-gardens of the Antiguan houses were especially gorgeous, and Henry, who was as sensitive as Audubon the naturalist to floral beauty, was enchanted by the scarlet cordias, and the saffron and crimson fences of hibiscus, and the massy radiance of tropical leaves. The gardens, he decided, were the antithesis of the cool water-colour gardens of England : the lilac jessamines hung in purple wreaths beside him, the fleshy American aloe (that inflexible cactus that before death bursts out into a thousand yellow aromatic blooms), stood rigidly pointing upwards beneath the festooned gigantic trees. On the road that winds round Brimstone Hill in St. Christopher's, he came upon a complete grove of the seaside grape. The unripe yellow fruit, something like a gooseberry but also something like a pippin, hung in clusters upon every branch, nestling amongst its round large leaves. The varied scenes stirred him to impromptu verses, addressed to the Caribbean :

> Beautiful islands ! where the green
> Which Nature wears was never seen
> 'Neath zone of Europe ; —where the hue,
> Of sea and heaven is such a blue
> As England dreams not ; where the night
> Is all irradiate with the light
> Of stars like moons which, hung on high,
> Breathe and quiver in the sky . . .
> Your sky-like seas, your sea-like skies,
> Your green bananas' giant leaves,
> Your golden canes in arrowy sheaves,
> Your palms which never die but stand,
> Immortal sea-marks on the strand. . . .

He continued for twenty-eight lines.

When the Coleridges came to the Islands, the Emancipation Controversy was still going strong. Various bills for the abolition of Slavery, a subject first brought up in the House of Commons two years before the outbreak of the French Revolution, had been produced and rejected. The partisans of the planters on the one hand, of the idealised negroes on the other, squabbled fiercely. In a sensible final chapter of his book, Henry Coleridge reviewed the problem without notice-

4

able bias. His judgments, he supposed, could please nobody, for he criticised in turn the abolitionists and their opponents the planters ; the Home Government ; the island legislatures; and finally the slaves themselves. Slavery, in his view, was a bad thing : but immediate abolition was worse. The slaves were better treated than London abolitionists conceived ; though far less well than many creoles proclaimed. He felt (and surely the bishop agreed with him) that what the slaves needed was a " moral stimulus," and this could only be provided by improved education, by " amendment of the existing details " of slavery, and by fixing freedom at a market price. It was this part of the book that interested his uncle Samuel Taylor Coleridge and his friend Southey : this was the excellent sense into which the latter had said Henry " saddened." But like many persons of his temperament, Henry Coleridge was apt to run headlong to conclusions : and with all his sensibility he was severe rather than humane. An excellent example is afforded by his advocacy of the tread-mill.

As well as churches, chapels and graveyards, each island held two other places of professional interest to the Bishop: the court-house and the jail. Now in the capital of St. Vincent island, the legislature had constructed a most excellent example of the West Indian jail ; but the Coleridges were " disgusted " to find that convict and runaway slaves were worked in chain-gangs in the streets. " Not," Henry explains, " that any bodily pain was occasioned by the fetters ; they were too light for that " ; it was rather that the custom " must wantonly wound the feelings of every Englishman . . . must be utterly useless to the public, and unspeakably injurious to the moral system of the wretched individual." Why, when St. Vincent's legislature handsomely voted forty-two thousand pounds for a new church, had they not deducted five hundred for a treadwheel ? The slave chained in the street, argued Henry, does not perform one hour's work of a British rustic in a whole day : " but will he, nill he, he would effect something more on the steps of the Brixton staircase." It was the same in Bridgetown, Barbados: the jail was infamous, and the

prisoners were herded together. Bishop Coleridge immediately appointed a " very deserving young clergyman of the
name of Packer " to attend to the prisoners : but his secretary
suggested that what the prison also needed was a " capacious
treadwheel." The treadwheel could be made of pitch-pine
and need not be very costly : indeed such was " the mild
influence of this blessed invention " that within a year the
money spent would be saved by a reduction in jail expenditure.
Whether somebody took action on Henry Coleridge's sugges-
tion we do not know ; but sure enough a large treadwheel was
soon installed in Bridgetown jail. Leaping eleven years we
may get a glimpse of this great wheel as it revolves slowly
beneath the blistered and bloodstained feet of negro prisoners.
In October 1836 a small but very determined party of members
of the Society of Friends embarked at Falmouth in the *Skylark*
packet and landed a month later on the shores of Carlisle Bay.
The suspicions of the Quakers had been aroused by the latest
Parliamentary Report on the progress of Abolition ; it almost
seemed, when you read this ambiguous document, that it had
" emanated from a tribunal in which the accused parties were
themselves judges." The little Quaker commission set to
work with characteristic energy and speed: Dr. Lloyd and
Mr. Scoble were at once dispatched to Bridgetown jail. Here,
after investigating the punishment of stone-breaking, they
shouldered their way into the chamber in which the dreaded
pitch-pine treadwheel stood. The wheel was going round
as they reached it : fifteen negroes, some of them young boys,
were on it, and those who were too weak to stand had been
strapped into an upright position. One and all were cruelly
and relentlessly flogged with the cat. Later in the day the
Quaker gentlemen again visited the wheel : this time mulatto
girls and women, with shaven heads and coarse cloth trousers,
were undergoing the torture. Enquiry showed that the
women (who were also flogged until they bled) were put upon
the treadmill for seven ten-minute periods a day. To the
Quakers, the Bridgetown treadwheel was one of the most
appalling of the many horrible and inhuman sights they saw in
the islands : and to think that only thirty yards from the

treadwheel building the Barbados legislature was holding its ancient sessions, almost within earshot of the convicts' groans. But if the cries of the treadmill's victims may have been audible in a building thirty yards away, they certainly could not cross three thousand miles of ocean to the study in Chester Place, Regent's Park, in which Henry Nelson Coleridge sat comfortably editing his uncle's literary remains.

When Cashel came over from his cottage in the mornings to his breakfast in Government House, the convicts were already at work in the gardens. This drove of twenty Indian and negro prisoners, with shining faces and cotton shorts, wandered all day about the lawns in charge of a stout negro policeman. In a day, perhaps, they did as little as an English rustic in an hour : but they seemed almost contented as they trailed vaguely about the pathways, impervious to the noonday sun. Here at least, thought Cashel, is one improvement in a hundred years. He came into direct contact with these prisoners when it was necessary (as it so often was) to shift furniture inside Government House. They were particularly bad at lifting big pieces of furniture ; particularly inane and careless. They thought it very funny when a bedstead got jammed in the doorway of the Prince of Wales' Bedroom, or a table seemed about to tumble down the stairs. Cashel, when he was alone with them, thought it was rather funny too. He liked the grins of the convicts as much as he disliked their strong smell, but he found it hard to understand their jabbering and their unshaped words. At such moments he felt in complete accord with Henry Coleridge's final verdict on *Six Months in the West Indies* : where, summing up the pains and the pleasures of life in the islands he wrote that the chief disadvantages were " perspiration, mosquitoes, and the yawny-drawly way in which the men converse."

Plantain Trees in the West Indies

Sir Walter Raleigh

Chapter Five

A SPRING-BOARD FOR ELDORADO

1595

Tell Fortune of her blindness,
Tell Nature of decay.
SIR W. RALEIGH : *The Lie*

" PARROTS ! "

Somebody pointed upwards. Gingerly shifting his position in the motor-boat, Cashel followed their gaze. He was just in time to see a string of small birds skimming the tops of the trees beside the lake. The birds seemed mere grains of colour flung into the high wide sky, and even the colour could not be identified they went so fast. It was a flash of plumage, that was all : it might have been lemon-yellow or apple-green, flame-coloured or turquoise. Before you could decide they had scattered away over the forests.

Cashel put on his sun-glasses again and resumed his survey of the lake. Although it seemed to him as grand and mysterious as any inland sea in darkest Africa he knew it to be of artificial and quite recent construction, a giant reservoir formed from a natural valley in the hills. This did not mean that it was near a town or easy of access. Approached by a long and difficult road that had been blasted through the hill-sides, the lake in fact lay isolated amidst dense and steamy forest. The surface of the lake was without a ripple and looked black. The sky was blue but very far away above the treetops. The trees were very vivid green and seemed abnormally tall, shutting in the lake on all sides with their curtains of creeper that made a solid and motionless wall. The only movement upon the lake appeared to be the birds that darted over it, the only noises the tumbling of a distant waterfall and the impatient ticking of the boat-engine, which somebody kept switching on and off.

That the lake had been so recently a valley gave it an

additional majesty in Cashel's eyes. He liked to fancy that they were floating above the waving branches of a drowned forest. And as the boat carried them slowly round the margin of the lake, past reed-beds and tunnels of greenery on the banks, past stream-courses and rotting logs, the scene became increasingly unreal to him. Far away across the water stood the bungalow of the reservoir keeper. Near it the long smooth Packard lay lazily in the shade of a twisted tree, and white-uniformed footmen were unpacking luncheon-baskets from the Ford van. But these signs of comparatively normal life were too frail to counterbalance the sensations that the forest, lake and sky were producing in Cashel. Was it beautiful or grand or frightening ? Or was it, he wondered as he peered over the boat's side into the dark water, infinitely sad ? He had already noticed in Trinidad, though without being able to explain it, the peculiar melancholy of tropical nature. It is not the temporal sadness of the English land-scape. It has nothing to do with a sense of passing time. It is something inhuman and eternal that you could sense even amongst the orderly trees in the Botanic Garden, and which in the High Woods and about this lake was far more strong. The little boat with its flat cotton cushions, its five occupants, the litter of parasols, cameras and field-glasses, seemed marooned upon some stretch of inky water, remote forever from the known world.

With a faint but strident cry and a flurry of wings a second lot of parrots burst from the treetops and passed in uneven flight across the lake.

" We saw birds of all colours, some carnation, some crimson, orange tawny, purple, green, watched and of all other sorts . . . and still as we rowed the deer came down feeding by the water's side."

Already in the summer of 1595 Raleigh's Guiana expedi-tion was ending in failure. He had left his ships in Trinidad, and set out over the Gulf of Paria for the sandy channels of the Orinoco delta with his captains and one hundred men, carried in one barge, one gallego, the boat of the *Lion's Whelp* and two wherries. Soon they had penetrated the mangrove swamps of the delta and were drawing up the wide pale river between the silent forest banks. At last they were upon the highway to Eldorado, that mythical kingdom for which the Spaniards had been searching sixty years. Like the Spaniards before them they were disappointed in their search : they did not find Eldorado. What they did find up the Orinoco were many curiosities : Indians who dwelt in trees, or crowned their kings' skeletons, or drank bones powdered in wine : a blue metalline stone (which Raleigh recognised as steel ore), white cranes and red herons, crocodiles, but nothing to justify the expedition in English eyes. Hard-headed shareholders in the enterprise—Cecil and the rest—were unlikely to be satisfied by tales of tortoise eggs, and specimens of rock that glinted like silver but equally like gold. Yet although he did not find Eldorado or its glittering capital Manoa, and although he came back to England without having annexed Guiana to the Tudor crown, Sir Walter Raleigh was more certain than ever that up the Orinoco river lay a land of promise for his compatriots. Home in England, in answer to hostile criticism, he put his case before the world by writing the *Discovery of Guiana*.

The opening chapters of the *Discovery* seem a medley of Spanish-Indian names : Orciones, Cuzco, Caximalca, Guiana-capa : it was tempting to Cashel to read them out loud, a cataract of syllables—Maracabo, Moriquito, Caramanata, Barquiesemeta, Tunio, Mozo, Popayan, Santa Fe de Bogota. But Raleigh was not writing for the dilettante, and in these early chapters he is concerned to develop his main thesis—that there is only one way to destroy the menace presented by Philip of Spain. The English were not aware that the decline of Spain had already set in ; to contemporaries the Armada victory did not seem so final as modern schoolboys have been taught to think, and writing towards the end of the 'nineties, Raleigh felt that Spanish power was still on the increase. "If we now . . . consider how many kingdoms he hath endangered, how many armies, garrisons and navies he hath and doth maintain ; the great losses which he hath repaired . . . yet notwithstanding he beginneth again, like a storm, to

threaten shipwreck to us all." And whence, he asks, does
Spanish strength come ? " Not from the trades of sacks and
Seville oranges ", but from the Indian gold. It was at the
mineheads, where the chained negroes and the sweating
Indians toiled, that the flow of ingots to Spain must be stopped.
In his turret room above the Thames in Durham Palace,
Raleigh sat studying each account of the New World on which
he could lay his hands. From the flimsy material of English
and Spanish wanderers' reports, concoctions more of rumour
than of fact, he tried to build a precise geographical hypothesis.
In the end he fancied that he knew the exact position of
Eldorado, locating it upon the shores of Lake Parima in
Guiana, a conjecture accepted by posterity until disproved by
Von Humboldt in the last century.

Raleigh's aims in his expedition were not coloured by a
youthful romanticism like that of Dudley. He was hard-
headed and tough ; and he intended to investigate the chances
for a later onslaught on Spain in Latin America, to make
money for himself and his backers, and to win again the
Queen's favour by offering her the "mighty, rich and beautiful
empire of Guiana." Once subject to the English throne, this
kingdom would put the English on a footing of financial
equality with Spain : " lord of more gold . . . of more cities
and people " than either Philip the Second or the Great Turk,
the Queen of England would then be able to dominate the
world. But Raleigh was peering into a future still very far
away. On an eastern horizon too distant for even his penetrating vision flashed the aigrettes and trampled the elephants
of Imperial Jubilee.

Raleigh left England in February 1595. Unlike Robert
Dudley (whose ships were even then approaching the shores of
Trinidad), he held a royal commission, though it was a coldly
worded document. He had not been restored to favour before
he sailed, and many people, including his wife, had tried to
stop the expedition altogether. Lady Raleigh had written
urgently to Cecil, in one of those elaborate epistles that her
generation were taught to construct, begging him to aid her
husband " draw sure water towards the east " rather than

" help him forward towards the sunset. Every month," she observed, " hath his flower, and every season his contentment, and you great counsellors are so full of new counsels as you are steady in nothing ; but we poor souls that hath bought sorrow at a high price, desire . . . the same misfortune we hold, fearing alterations will but multiply misery." " I humbly beseech you," she ended more directly, " rather stay him than further him." But Eldorado with its plates of gold and its jewel-houses shimmered too bright.

Having survived these intrigues, and assembled his followers—officers, gentlemen, soldiers and volunteers, one hundred in all—Raleigh was next opposed by contrary weather : " this wind breaks my heart ; " it was impossible to set sail. But when at length the wind changed, they got quickly under way, blown at first down to the Canary Islands and then on to Teneriffe and so out across the southern sea. Aubrey records the fact that Raleigh employed his leisure aboard ship by intellectual work. A trunk of books stood in his cabin, beside the green silk bed supported upon dolphins' heads in gilded wood. Here he would sit with his maps and his travellers' journals, feeding his optimism on Diego de Ordaz' account of the unimaginable wealth of Manoa City in the year 1531. Like all his educated contemporaries Raleigh had dabbled in the cold moonswept waters of antique mythology. Perhaps he forgot how purely legendary is the tale of Danae and her sudden shower of gold.

Of all the travellers in the archbishop's library Cashel liked Raleigh the least. Raleigh's attitude to his adventures was tough and worldly : and his character seemed too complicated and had too many facets. In the High Renaissance manner he was not only an imperialist and an explorer : he was also a scholar, a soldier, a courtier and a poet : and it was only in the last capacity that Cashel found him tolerable. Probably because Raleigh felt the printing of verse to be both unnecessary and vulgar, his position as a minor Elizabethan poet rested for three centuries upon tradition. The remains of his authentic verse has recently been carefully collated, and certain of his poems that have long masqueraded under other people's names have been restored to their author :

> Give me my scallop shell of quiet,
> My staff of faith to walk upon,
> My scrip of joy, immortal diet,
> My bottle of salvation ;
> My gown of glory, hope's true gage,
> And thus I'll take my pilgrimage.

> Blood must be my body's balmer,
> No other balm will there be given,
> Whilst my soul, like a white palmer,
> Travels to the land of heaven,
> Over the silver mountains,
> Where spring the nectar fountains.

Cashel used to feel how much these lines were the antithesis not merely of modern English life in the tropics but also of the high-keyed religious spirit of the old Spanish colonial world.

The exploratory character of Raleigh's venture, his intention to scout out the empire of Guiana for future attack, made Trinidad his first goal. Trinidad at this time was occupied by the Spaniards in a half-hearted way ; they too regarded the island merely as a stepping-stone to the mythical swampland kingdoms of the continent. Robert Dudley had avoided a brush up with the Spanish garrison of the mud town of San Josef, but Raleigh knew that in the Spanish governor of the island he would find an expert in American adventure. Antonio de Berrio was an elderly and cultured Spaniard who had married the heiress to almost unlimited estates in the New World. When young he had served King Philip in Italy and in the Netherlands : and then he had turned to his inheritance across the Atlantic, and spent the remainder of his life and all his hopes and energies in searching for Eldorado. It had cost him more than he gained. He squandered money and men up the Orinoco river, and journeyed and fought despairingly to find Manoa. Sometimes he killed Indians, sometimes he allied himself with them. Like all the Spanish administrators in the New World he squabbled with his compatriots, driven to fury by his struggles and his disappointments, and agued by the damp heat. Occasionally he would send back some offering to the King of Spain—a wrought gold image taken from the Indians, or some tropical curiosity. But as the years passed on the Main he acquired experience and knowledge : and these were things which Raleigh, who had only written information and academic theories, required. At this moment, Berrio was living in Trinidad, in the town which he had ordered Domingo de Vera to build in the jungle around the Franciscan's wooden cross. This was the town that Raleigh must capture : this was the town he determined, as a vengeance, to destroy. He was certain that Berrio was personally responsible for the murder of some English sailors a year before : the men had guilelessly accepted a Spanish invitation to hunt in the forests and their simplicity had quickly cost them their lives. This piece of treachery infuriated Walter Raleigh, who characteristically considered that it could only be repaid in precisely the same coin.

The ships arrived at Punto de Gallo in Trinidad on March 22nd. Robert Dudley's fleet had left a few hours before. For the first five days after his arrival, Raleigh let his ships lie at the south of the island, while he made a slow inspection of the coast from his barge, and drew a sketch-map of the rivers and watering-places which he sent to Lord Henry Howard. From a boat low on the water, Trinidad appears to rise majestically from the sea : you get an impression of tree-trunks and creepers, creepers and tree-trunks, rank on rank of heavy untidy foliage like a cheap tapestry scene. It was along this tangled seashore that the barge was daily rowed : and seated in it a bent, eager figure like a Hilliard, a tall man of forty in a shirt of embroidered linen, on his black curly head a wide felt hat that shielded from the sun's rays his dark bearded face, with its high oblong forehead and " sour-lidded . . . pig eye."

After five days the ships moved on to Port of Spain (or as the Indians called it, Conquerabia), but still the Spaniards showed no sign of life, and still Raleigh continued his circumspect journeys in his barge. As he went he sampled the fruits and fishes of the tropics, and particularly liked the salt-tasting tiny oysters from the fetid Caroni swamp. At length the English came upon some Spanish civilians, who seemed inclined to trade. A number of them came aboard the ships one evening, to buy linen and look at English goods. Here was the opporunity for which Raleigh had waited. He entertained them carefully, giving them wine which they had been without many years and leading them on to talk of Guiana. He deliberately created the impression that he had no wish to go to Guiana, and was in fact bound for the relief of his own Virginian colony; until encouraged by the wine and by his candour they told him all they knew. He had been warned by Indians of impending reinforcements for the Spanish garrison, and he realised that if he wanted to capture Berrio and destroy San Josef he must do it now. The Spaniards who were his guests he killed : and then landing with one of his captains and a hundred men, he crept along the coast in the darkness of the following morning, and surprising the guard outside San Josef put them to the sword. By daybreak he had captured the tapia town, while a priest and the women of the little colony fled into the woods, to escape later to Margarita with their tale of slaughter. He took Berrio himself prisoner, sending him back to the English ships and then ("at the instance," he explains, "of the Indians ") he fired the town which, with such pious pageantry, Vera had founded three years before. The tapia huts flamed merrily in the light of the dawn, and the smoke from the little church curled upwards, black against the emerald tree branches and the brown Laventille Hills.

Raleigh found in Berrio a disillusioned and pessimistic person. He had lost all faith in Eldorado. He lacked geographical curiosity. He seemed unable to distinguish east from west. He knew that more than one hundred rivers were tributary to the Orinoco but could he name any of these ? No. And he could not describe the land through which the great river flowed. To Raleigh's precise mind this vagueness was maddening ; and he soon made it clear that Berrio would have a chance of refreshing his mind upon the hydrography of the American continent. He explained to the unfortunate old man that he was expected to accompany the English in a wherry, a gallego or a barge. Soon, with a hundred men, his captains and this elderly Spanish gentleman,

View from the Laventille Hills, Trinidad

The North Coast, Trinidad

[*From Kingsley's "At Last,"* 1870

A Sea-beach in Trinidad

[*From Kingsley's "At Last,"* 1870

The Dragons Mouths, Trinidad

Sir Walter Raleigh was setting off across the Gulf of Paria to the Orinoco river mouth.

Cashel was not fond of going out upon the glassy surface of the Gulf of Paria. He had his reasons. From the North-West corner of Trinidad stretches a chain of tiny islands, like an accusing arm, pointing at the continent. These islets, which create the dangerous channels called (after Columbus) the Dragons Mouths are encrusted with the week-end villas of magnates from Port of Spain—all save one, the greenest, the most beautiful, Chacachacare Island, the site of the leper settlement of Trinidad. It was to this place (little frequented by Trinidad people) that Cashel was taken in a motor-launch soon after his arrival in Port of Spain. He sat back in the launch on the outward journey, enraptured by the morning panorama of small tree-tufted islands in the olive sea, of white waves spouting up over pebbly beaches, under a blazing sun. On the water pelicans bobbed solemnly like celluloid toys. When they reached Chacachacare the boat was moored in a shallow bay, and after a bathe in the green sea-water they lunched from picnic baskets in one of those peeling, empty rest-houses that Cashel already recognised as a peculiarity of British administration in the tropics. On the way back that evening, however, the motor-launch (which was of local design and sat up on the water with the elegance of a handsome cab) was caught smack on in a sudden, horrible squall. Like everyone else, as the boat was wrenched from side to side, and the negroes, who are not born seamen, tugged at the wheel, Cashel supposed they were about to upset. Unlike everyone else he had no theory about what the boatmen should not do, no recipe against disaster. He only noted mentally that if they ever survived this alive it might be better not to venture out into the Gulf of Paria in such a launch again. The leper island had been exquisite, but was it worth risking a drowning to see ?

Although Raleigh's first Guiana expedition had proved utterly fruitless, he had left a legend behind him. A born propagandist, he had applied himself vigorously to the task of interesting the Indians of Trinidad in England and the English Queen. Queen Elizabeth, he explained, by an interpreter, was the great Cassique of the North. Under her rule lived happily more princelings than there were trees in Trinidad. The open, and more, the victorious enemy of Spain, she had delivered Europe from the Spanish yoke, and now " all the coast of the northern world " freed " from their servitude " she planned a similar liberation for the Americas. Raleigh, in fact, was her chosen emissary, selected to free the Indians. These palpable lies met with a great reception. " I showed them Her Majesty's picture, which they so admired and honoured as it had been easy to have brought them idolatrous thereof." The Indians devised a title for the Queen of England—*Elizabeta Cassipuna Aquerewani*—" which is as much as Elizabeth the great princess or greatest commander." And just as he took care to distort his royal mistress to proportions the Indians could understand, so Raleigh later simplified the complexities of the native tribal systems for his European audience. " The kings of the borders " had willingly become Elizabeth's vassals ; and of course, as he wrote many years later to Lord Carew, their allegiance had been inherited by James the First.

Chapter Six

ADVENTURES OF A NAVAL SURGEON

1808

> The boat is chafing at our long delay,
> And we must leave too soon
> The spicy sea-pinks and the inborne spray,
> The tawny sands, the moon.
>
> JOHN DAVIDSON : *Song*

ONE EVENING TOWARDS the end of August, 1808, an Englishman was riding peacefully down the road to Grandbourg, chief
town of the small island of Marie Galante. As he went along
he admired the oranges and the mammy-apple trees, and the
fine neat scenery which made him think of an English country
seat or of Kew Gardens. It was some time since he had seen
either : for one year in charge of the Naval Hospital at
Bridgetown, Barbados had been followed by another aboard
the sloop *Nimrod*, hunting for French men-of-war and privateers in the Mona Channel, the strip of water between Costa
Rica and Puerto Rico, and sailing down the white mud coast
of Surinam to Parimaribo ; and now since three days ago he
was resident surgeon to the garrison in the pestilence-infested
island of Marie Gallante.

Marie Galante had only lately been occupied by the
English, who had seized it as a base for future operations
against Guadaloupe. The capture of the island had been
cleverly effected : the English commander chose the night of
the annual carnival to launch his attack, and the English
marines arrived to find many of the French inhabitants still
strutting the streets in their carnival costumes. The French,
however, had excellent manners and submitted to the occupation with a very good grace. They even seemed to take an
especial interest in the welfare of the English marines, supply-
ing them liberally with raw rum.

Nobody who knew Marie Galante had ever supposed it to

have a healthy climate. The barracks into which the English troops were moved were situated in the most swampy quarter of the swamp-encircled town. The citizens of Grandbourg watched with polite interest as the English commander paraded his garrison twice daily, drilled them in the sun each afternoon, and instituted two field-days a week. They continued their welcome gifts of rum. The invasion had taken place in early spring ; by May the men began to suffer from ulcers ; in June they were dying of fever in twenty-four hours ; at the beginning of August the officers succumbed and eight died within a fortnight ; the garrison was reduced to two hundred men, of whom one hundred and sixty were in hospital. Four medical officers had died while attending the stricken garrison. A fifth was accordingly appointed by the Commander-in-Chief of the West Indies station. The name of this officer, who had been snatched unwilling from a homeward-bound convoy, was Mr. John Waller.

As he was passing a house upon the road to Grandbourg, his mind divided between Kew Gardens and the mortality at the country hospitals which he had just left, Mr. Waller was stopped unexpectedly. A French planter had come out of the house into the highway, followed by a troop of French ladies. They earnestly invited him to step into the house for a few moments, which he felt himself obliged in common courtesy to do. Inside he was treated with the greatest consideration and the ladies revealed that they had a favour to ask. Could the Englishman join them at breakfast the next morning ? An open air breakfast : they had engaged a number of their friends to come with them, and all that they needed to complete the party were some of the English officers. When Mr. Waller got back to Grandbourg would he persuade as many of his brother officers as he could to come to the breakfast with him ? And in particular would he bring the Adjutant, Mr. Jones ? They pointed out how little excuse there was for him to refuse them, since he rode each morning by their house. Waller was in fact far too busy to wish to join them, but " there is something so persuasive in the eloquence of a French lady, and she meets all your objections with so many

accommodating arrangements that . . . I consented to breakfast with them." At this they let him go, and seeing him on to
his horse again they stood watching him as he rode off in the
direction of Grandbourg beneath the evening sky.

Waller passed on the invitation to the Adjutant, and
arranged that they should proceed together to the rendezvous,
which had been fixed for eight o'clock. It was already eight,
however, before Waller had finished his round of the town
hospitals the next morning. On returning to his lodging he
found that Mr. Jones had set off alone for the picnic, riding
Waller's own horse, but taking with him a negro who was to
bring the horse back so that the surgeon should follow on.
A little piqued, and extremely busy, Waller decided to abandon
the picnic party, and going over to the Priest's House took
breakfast with the English Governor. In doing this he
avoided an unpleasant adventure. The house of the planter
lay two miles out of Grandbourg, and was reached by a road
through a very beautiful ravine, along which the lime and the
lemon tree grew wild in great profusion. The adjutant's horse
trotted slowly along ; the adjutant was " wrapt in deep
reflection which the scenery alone was well calculated to
inspire." So preoccupied was he that he did not notice when
he was challenged by a sentry, nor, even more odd, that the
sentry wore French uniform. The challenge was several
times repeated, and then the sentry fired. The ball knocked
off the adjutant's hat ; and Mr. Jones awoke suddenly to find
himself a few yards from the breakfast party, which consisted
of a great number of French officers and " many of the most
respectable inhabitants of the island " seated upon the ground
" making a sumptuous breakfast under the shade of the trees."
The friends the English officers had been asked to meet were
in fact part of a force of one hundred and twenty Frenchmen
from Guadaloupe, landed the previous night in the Bay of St.
Louis.

The French gentry of Marie Galante were at this period a
mixed batch. Many of them were refugees from the Revolution, the dismayed remnants of the Bourbon aristocracy.
Others were men who had held power during the years of the

5

Terror, and had in their turn fled, like their victims before
them, to the safety of the sugar islands and the calm life of the
Antilles.   It was from both these elements that the breakfast
party was drawn.   And how well one can picture this early
morning *fête champetre* : the officers and the ladies seated
carelessly upon the ground amongst the nodding tropical
grasses, the threads of early morning sunlight falling through
the canopy of foliage overhead, around them and above them
the olive-green and emerald-green, the pale sharp green and the
soft laurel-coloured leaves quivering, the white flowers and the
scarlet flowers, and the wild lime trees.   Around them is
spread the breakfast (Waller had found the people of Marie
Galante to be epicures ; but then he, too, had suffered under
the English colonials' mutton chops) : baskets of glistening
fruits, long loaves of bread swathed in napkins, cold fowl and
pies, flagons of light wine.   For one moment the ladies and
gentlemen raise their heads, startled by the sentry's shot: the
next this Lancret gathering is shocked and shattered as the
English adjutant, at last aware that he has walked into an
ambuscade, vaults his horse over the " breakfast apparatus,"
dashes into the thicket and disappears.   Their attempt, by
kidnapping the English officers, to leave the garrison denuded,
had failed ; and " the French had nothing to do but to finish
their breakfast with all possible despatch, and proceed at once
on the attack."

Galloping back to Grandbourg, Mr. Jones arrived at the
Governor's house, where he found the staff officers eating, and
announced the French attack.   Simultaneously the sentry at
the gate perceived an advancing column with bayonets not
a mile away ; and the frigate *Circe* which lay out in the bay,
sighted a second column and fired a warning gun.   No time
was to be lost.   Determined to fight for Grandbourg against
seemingly hopeless odds, the Governor decided to do so from
a tiny fort within the town.   One wall of this fort formed one
side of a small *place*, grass-grown, with two lines of trees along
it, rows of houses forming the three other sides.   Basing his
sickly forces upon the fort the Governor, accompanied by
Waller and the other officers, advanced to the Savannah, there

to meet the French. They arrived in time to see a bold counter-attack made by the British marines. Meanwhile the frigate in the Bay was sending boatloads of sailors ashore—though to the almost triumphant French a few English reinforcements did not seem likely to prevent a French victory. The exchange of fire upon the Savannah continued all day, the French beating *pas de charge* upon their drums, and in the afternoon the French commander asked the English to surrender. To put his demand with proper dignity, the rash officer stepped into the very centre of the square *place* before the fort ; his men, who should have followed him, retired to the houses that faced upon it ; and the British marines, unrestrained by their officers' orders, shot him dead. With him fell his sergeant and his drummer. The French morale gave way. In spite of superiority in numbers and in arms, in spite of their advantage in surprise, the French retreated. By the end of the next day all had been either captured or driven from the island.

The incident which had begun so picturesquely with the *al fresco* breakfast was closed. The estates of some of the more prominent supporters of the attempt against the English were sequestrated, but restored to their owners within the year. Amongst the casualties after the battle the English were sorry to find an old negress, who, fascinated by the spectacle of the frigate's guns spluttering in the Bay, had stood watching at an open window until a cannon-ball had carried off her head. Waller returned to the less exciting work of inspecting the town and country hospitals, comforting himself for the French ladies' perfidy by the theory that they had asked him to breakfast in order to preserve his life.

This was the episode in Waller's narrative that Cashel liked best. The whole journal, which is one of activity and of adventure, pleased him. After the enthusiasm of Victorian sightseers, he found Waller simple and level-headed, his pages filled with facts about French privateers—*La Vaillante, La Bien Aimée*—or navigation in the Leeward Islands, the bleakness of the black Virgin Gordas or the prosperity of Surinam.

There was in addition a charming romanticism in Waller's nature, a sensitivity that made him walk by moonlight in Barbadoes or sent him clambering up a perpendicular rock face to gaze upon the evening panorama of Porto Rico and St. Thomas and the blue island-studded channel in between. He responded quickly and unself-consciously to any form of beauty : the olive humming-birds dipping about the bugle-shaped Barbadoes Pride, the " gay, green and polished " palm-trees, the lizards streaked with gold and azure, a lovely negro child, a majestic ravine, the perfect shape and workmanship of the big gold Spanish doubloons.

Cashel himself did not visit the French islands until he was leaving the West Indies for good, on his way home. It was then that Martinique and Guadaloupe seized upon his imagination as they had never done when he had read of them in books. Travelling by choice upon a small French steamboat —the passage-ways choked with baggage, the saloons filled with cumbrous Spanish nuns and with Dutch priests from Surinam—he had spent a single day in Martinique, being driven up and round the green cone of the volcano, and down to the grass-thick ruins of St. Pierre upon the further shore. He had spent another day at Guadaloupe. From each island he carried away a brilliant, a photographic impression of the traditions of Europe merged into the world of the tropics ; he could sense the contrast of colonial methods which Trollope had been so quick to see. Inevitably it was the departure from both places—his departure, perhaps forever, from the West Indies—that stayed most vividly in his mind. Martinique they had left amid scenes of unexampled chaos : late arrivals scuffled up the gangplank as the ship's bell rang ; cabin trunks were hurled on to the decks ; hooters were blown ; stout negresses scurried hither and thither along the quay ; unauthorised persons were suddenly refused permission to leave the ship, while other travellers with authentic tickets were rigorously prevented from boarding it at all. When the chaos seemed at its height the ship's bilges were opened, and filthy mango-stones, fish heads and banana skins spewed out upon the gesturing crowds along the quay. It was a very different departure from the melancholy leave-takings at Guadaloupe. There, at Pointe-à-Pitre everyone was crying. The crowds upon the quayside were silent. The afternoon was drawing in. Cramped against the ship's rails, Cashel strove passionately to fix each detail into his memory. He determined to pick upon some single person or object and to rivet his attention upon that. Near the water's edge, in front of the crowd which was itself formed up in front of the great customs sheds stood an old, old negress, a small bent figure with an orange and black cloth tied round her head, and a full black and white chintz skirt ; she was sobbing into a white handkerchief, an old woman from a West Indian colour-print. As the ship slipped slowly away from the quay Cashel watched her. Small as she was to begin with, her figure became gradually smaller, dwindling to a mere patch of black, and then to a smudge of grey. The whole crowd, into which she had now faded, and the big warehouses that had seemed to tower above them were shrinking, shrinking. At length, irresistibly, Cashel put out his hand at arm's length : it covered the whole quay, and the whole shore, and soon the whole sea-front of Pointe a Pitre and the low hills behind it, and the gap in the ground where the Rivière Salee runs. Cashel knew then that he had seen the end of the West Indies, and as the ship put out to sea he went and stood in the stern and gazed back at Guadaloupe. In an hour or two the sun began to set : the arc of the sky became ochre, with black clouds piled solidly within it, and the flat black island of Guadaloupe already far, far away. A warm tropical wind was blowing gently over the decks. Night fell. Soon all that remained to be seen of the West Indies was a light that flashed mechanically on the horizon. What light is that ? Cashel asked a fellow-passenger.

" Ça ? Mais ça c'est le phare de Marie Galante."

After his time in the islands, Waller's first glimpse of England was terribly disappointing. He landed at Portsmouth, and found this town and Porchester Castle and even more the country lying on either hand of the London road

extraordinarily meagre ; compared with the plumy forests of
Dominica the beautiful seat of Mount Edgecumbe was
nothing but a wilderness.   The French Creole prisoners he
was escorting, who had never seen Europe before, were not
impressed.   And yet however tame the English landscape
might appear, Waller felt himself amply compensated by the
vitality and intelligent aspect of his compatriots.   He reflected
that their animated faces formed a contrast to any he had seen
in the Antilles.

Although he found time in the Caribbean both for criticism
and admiration, Waller was essentially an active and busy man.
He lived for a whole year in Barbados and for some months
on Marie Galante ; but his narrative is chiefly one of sea-
adventure.   There is nothing stuffy about his experiences :
he was not shut into Government Houses, nor driven in hot
carriages along parched roads.   On shore he walked or rode ;
but he was happiest roving with the *Nimrod* amongst the
Leeward Islands, looking at the solitary rocks that were some
of them like tables or hats or coffins, swooping down into
sheltered harbours where towns like Roseau or Christiansandt
lay neat and peaceful at the foot of green hills.   They were
constantly passing Martinique and Santa Cruz, or lying
becalmed off the Saints in full sight of Guadaloupe and
Dominica.   There was always the hope of a French brig to
chase, seen in one channel, lost in the next.   There were
English schooners bound from Curaçao to Tortola, and great
mysterious convoys of tall ships that slipped by in the night.
There were coral reefs to be navigated.   There were dolphins
to be caught.   Cashel liked to picture the *Nimrod* skimming,
like a sloop in an Ackermann colour-print, across a tranquil
waveless sea, or tacking to a blustering wind.

The island that Waller seemed to like best was St. Thomas,
lately taken from the Danes and held by the British from 1807
to 1815.   The town of St. Thomas itself, previously called
Charlotte Amelia, had been burned out and only partly re-
built ; yet however " ungrateful " and " ruinous " when you
got on shore, the town was a place of especial beauty from the
sea.   Its bay was deep, and the houses lay clustered in a

Port of Spain, Trinidad, about 1850

The Carenage and St. George Town and Bay, Grenada

" noble kind of amphitheatre," mountains, cultivated to their summits, rising sheer at its back. On their first visit to St. Thomas they weighed anchor after a few hours in the harbour and ran down the coast to a watering-place, Black-rock, about ten miles to leeward of the town. Waller had stayed the night on shore and followed the ship down to Black-rock in the morning, in a small four-oared cutter. He found the watering-place to be at the bottom of a wild gully, with a mountain perpendicular above it. His time on his hands, he began to examine the trees and shrubs nearby, and had soon discovered a new kind of aloe, five foot high, with scarlet leaves and white and yellow blossoms ; another species grew to be twenty feet. The scented snake-wood, with white flowers like garden lilies, grew there in profusion. There were sour-sops, too, an acid antidote to thirst, and the crab-eyes from which the negroes got the small red peas they strung as necklaces of beads. There were quantities of wild pine plants, the flowers hanging carelessly about the bushes as though thrown down by the wind. The possibilities of the gully exhausted, Waller set out to climb the mountain by a mule-track he had spied along its side. As he went the heat became violent, and near the top he realised he could not go on. Looking down the mountain he saw a small house. To this he descended, very tired. It turned out to be the house on a sugar estate, occupied by a young manager and his wife, both Danes. They welcomed him most hospitably, giving him food and showing him over their sugar-works ; they even put him to bed to sleep for two hours. After dining with these new friends he was taken down the mountain by the manager. He found the watering of the ship continuing, men setting casks beneath the gushing, pellucid cascades. He went back to the ship for the night, and set off again the next afternoon to reach the topmost ridge of the mountain, though much fatigued. The prospect from the summit was rewarding : beneath him in the Bay the *Nimrod* rode at anchor like a toy, and her boats seemed specks floating on the water as they passed to and fro; the lofty ranges of Porto Rico hid the sunset ; the sea between that island and St. Thomas was studded with tiny islands.

To eastward towered the higher mountains of St. Thomas, their sides covered with fresh pale sugar cane. Enraptured by this panorama, he remained seated upon a crag until the sun had set and " the fainter light of the rising moon had sweetly tinged with a different hue each object around me." It was only then that he began to go down, making his way past the house to which he had been the day before. He found the little family in their gallery, " contemplating the scene ; " and joining them there, he sat eating fruit and gazing at the little islands, or " keys," amongst which ships were sailing in the moonlight. The little Danes were delighted to see him again, for he told them news of what was going on in the world. So sympathetic was their society, so splendid the view, that " it was not till I heard the report of the evening gun, rolling like thunder through the rocks beneath us, that I thought of returning. I then took leave, and descended to the bottom of the valley, where I found a boat waiting for me."

In the morning they beat up to St. Thomas, and within a week they were again at sea, sailing by the rocks called the Fallen City in the Virgin Gordas, navigating the passage between Sombrero and the isle of Anegada which is encircled by a treacherous reef.

Chapter Seven

FROUDACITY

1887

Oh palms grew high in Aves and fruits that shone like gold
And the celebris and parrots they were gorgeous to behold.
KINGSLEY : *The Lay of the Last Buccaneer*

A FIRST IMPRESSION of any place is seldom the same as a first sight of it. Cashel's first sight of Port of Spain was of a low quay decked out for an official welcome : a white-coated police band, pennoned launches, a strip of crimson carpet stretched on the yellow dust in the sunlight, a shuffling file of local notables shaking His Excellency's hand : in the background a serried, silent and watchful negro crowd. All this was too disjointed and too colourful to imprint itself upon the surface of his mind : the streets of shops through which the swift cars passed were equally presented to him in a blurred and jumbled form. So far there was no solidity or unity of vision : nothing he could place beside his original impression of the whole island, seen early that morning from the ship's deck, a calm series of smooth green hills rising from a clear sea. He knew that this impression of Trinidad would stay with him, for it had survived the fatal effects of diminishing perspective, as the motor-boat carried them to the shore, the distant island contours showing less smooth, until the hills seemed to erupt into a series of roads, houses, villages and trees and Trinidad became to his vision like life to that of the neurotic—disintegrated and too close. But Port of Spain was bewildering and unco-ordinated : each of his senses was assailed by clamorous novelty : and then, just as he was relinquishing the tussle, the car in which he was travelling passed the last villa and the final palmito, and emerged beside the Savannah which lay behind its iron railings large, flat and impersonal in the sweeping rain.

And so the wet Savannah became the pendant picture to the

green island ; and as the weeks went by the Savannah came to
occupy a paramount place in Cashel's conception of Trinidad.
It had a permanent quality alien to the rest of the tropical
landscape.   If you stood upon the verandah of the big ballroom, or of one of the bedrooms above it, you could look across
the formal garden, the bandstand and the railings to the road
and the savannah beyond ; and, though the flower-beds in the
garden seemed to change overnight (as the highly-coloured
blossoms unfolded with the speed of a parasol, or withered in
a moment on their juicy stalks) the tufted savannah grass was
always brown, and the dull prospect could be counted on to
look the same at any time and in any weather—Blackheath
devoid of dignity or associations.   Wherever you drove from
Government House—down to the shops, along to the barracks,
out to Maqueripe, or up the Belmont Circular Road—you
started off by passing the Savannah; and on certain occasions
—the Races or the King's Birthday—you drove through a gap
in the railings and on to savannah itself.   Bump, bump, bump
the car would jolt over the uneven coarse grassland, following
the flattened oval of the racecourse until the grandstand was
reached.   From the grandstand, with its back to the town and
the sea, you gained the mild satisfaction of seeing a familiar
view reversed, and looking out from the heart of the savannah
at the distant iron railings, the road, the formal garden, and the
egg-box verandahs of Government House.

The King's Birthday review took place at breakfast time.
They had erected a flagpole and a saluting base near the race-
track, and set out garden chairs in long lines for the officials
and their families.   The review was of the Colonial Police who
rode in white uniforms and white topees upon dark horses, and
of the island volunteers, who marched.   Plum-red feathers
fluttered on the topees of the officers.   The sun had risen over
the hills behind Government House, and shone down upon
the cavalcade with a fresh but gauzy light.   Like all such
functions in colonial life the parade was stirring and exciting,
but Cashel felt woefully out of place.   Physically as well as
mentally he was the wrong shape for these imperial displays:
the official photographs confirmed this belief, for he appeared

The Carenage, Island of Grenada

[*From a chalk drawing by Goodall in the National Portrait Gallery*

James Anthony Froude

in them a languid and indifferent figure, solitary in a throng of
solemn and sturdy functionaries.   He did not know what to
do with his hat on such occasions ; nor what to say to the
Anglican bishop ; nor to the Colonial Secretary's tiny daughter
who kept clutching at his hand.

It was just before sunset, at the close of a winter's day in
1887.   From the flagstaff which stood before the door of the
newly-built Government House the limp flag was being hauled
down.   Stumps had been drawn on the Savannah cricket-
pitch though on the ground itself people lingered, dawdling
across the grass in the orange evening.   Along the road
round the savannah many carriages were slowly moving, their
painted wheels revolving on the tarmacadam.   Languid
owners looked out at the prospect from the porches of their
villas, shaded by scented canopies of wisteria and bougainvilles.
In one particular carriage two men were seated : a distinguished citizen of Port of Spain, who owned a house facing the
Savannah, and an even more distinguished stranger from
England.   The stranger looked tall, although seated : and
his lined pallid face, greying black hair, black eyebrows and
brilliant eyes made an impressive effect.   His expression was
melancholy and disillusioned : but he looked about him with
amused attention, observing that the scene on the Savannah
put him in mind of Kensington Gardens on a Sunday.   The
circumference of the Savannah was then—as it is now—
supposed to be three miles : and before the carriage had completed the circuit, the sun had set, the fireflies had begun to
sparkle, and bats " swept and whistled " over their heads.
Set down at the gate of his host's villa, the stranger paused a
moment to gaze at the great palm tree which stood beside it,
its crown of leaves spiky against the sky, and a single dead
frond clashing on the stem in the night wind.

Froude had set out for the West Indies in a mood of grim
determination, tempered by his innate romanticism.   Until
his voyage to South Africa in the 'seventies he had cherished
a profound faith in the British imperial system.   His African
visit shook that faith ; and a journey to Australia some years

later shook it more violently yet. He had now embarked, at the age of sixty-eight, to examine with relentless curiosity the precise state of the oldest of British colonial possessions. What he found in the West Indies was so little to his taste that he gave his travel-book the sub-title *The Bow of Ulysses*: a graceful allusion to the neglectful methods of the British Colonial Office of his time. His book aroused the inevitable outcry in the Caribbean ; and evoked at least one sharp reply, *Froudacity* by a negro gentleman named Thomas. Froude's opinions on the West Indies were, of course, influenced by his relationship with Carlyle ; in Cheyne Row he had learned to add the Sage of Chelsea's loathing of democracy and popular government to his own natural conservatism. A lifetime spent in poring over Tudor documents had not helped to make him liberal ; and we may find finger-posts to his convictions in his whole-hearted admiration of Henry VIII, William Cecil and John Knox. He hated oratory and despised debate : and (so he tells us) as his ship, bound for Bridgetown, sped down the crumpled Portuguese coastline, followed by the snow-white gulls, he sat upon the deck pondering over the destruction of England and her Empire by orators and liberals. Not reform, but reaction, would be his solution for the West Indies, and he could have had no sympathy with Trollope's rosy dreams of coloured government. It was thus unfortunate that he arrived in the West Indies during a period of Home Rule agitation, and stepped ashore in Port of Spain three days before a mammoth meeting staged on the Savannah in favour of a new, free constitution. It was merely tactless that the organisers of the meeting should have rushed to him with an invitation to attend.

But there was another aspect of Froude's personality which we must take into account. This was a romantic passion for the sea. Homer, Hakluyt, any tale of seafaring adventure had fascinated him : a passion dating perhaps from his strange boyhood, when as a member of the ailing family of a Devonshire clergyman he had played with his brothers and sisters in the ruins of Dartington Hall, and watched first his mother and then six of her eight children die of consumption. Later, as an historian, he was unable to suppress his admiration for the English buccaneers, whom he rationalised as the " armed soldiers of the Reformation and avengers of humanity." A ship-board acquaintance who travelled back with him from the Cape in 1875 noticed that this " sad . . . tender . . . and usually cynical " man would light up and speak " with wonderful beauty of language " when relating the gallantry of some of his seafaring heroes of the Renaissance. As a young man he had once been asked to review a new edition of Hakluyt: and this article so fired two young contemporaries—Kingsley and Tennyson—that each sat down and wrote the one *Westward Ho* ! the other *The Last Voyage of the Renown*. It was with his mind full of his old friend Charles Kingsley that he had come to Trinidad : and as his ship steamed past the Bocas on the morning of his arrival, the rhythmic periods of the *Lay of the Last Buccaneer* had reverberated through his head :

> And the negro maids from Aves from bondage fast did flee,
> To welcome gallant sailors a sweeping in from sea.
>
> Oh sweet it was in Aves to hear the landward breeze,
> A swing with good tobacco in a net between the trees. . . .

And then on landing he had been met by the invitation from the constitution-mongers : and his mind had contracted again into disapproval, scepticism and distaste.

Replying that he was " greatly obliged by the compliment," but knew too little of their affairs to make his presence of any value to them, Froude went on to point out to the demonstrators that political changes were generally " little more than turns of a kaleidoscope : " a new pattern made of the same pieces : and with this caution he dismissed the matter. He turned once more from the " commonplace " to the " imaginative ; " submitting willingly to the charms of the Blue Basin waterfall, and the wonders of the Botanic Garden. When Trinidad politics once more intruded upon his consciousness in the form of the actual demonstration on the Savannah held under his very nose, he did again permit his thoughts to dwell briefly upon West Indian self-government. His conclusions

were shrewd to the point of cynicism, for to the oratorical
question " Why should not Trinidad govern itself as well as
Tasmania or New Zealand ? " he replied by merely posing
another query—" Do we or do we not intend to retain our
West Indian Islands under the sovereignty of the Queen ? "
With this telling rejoinder he contents his readers : stifling
their latent doubts upon the ideals of Port of Spain's citizens
by explaining that of the many thousand persons whom he saw
thronging the Savannah on the day of the Meeting, quite
more than half were there to watch the Governor batting in a
local cricket-match.

The same evening, Froude dined at Government House.
The Governor, Sir William Robinson, seemed to him " one of
those happy men whose constitution is superior to the climate;"
that is to say he could work all morning, play cricket or lawn
tennis all the afternoon and entertain " with sumptuous
hospitality " at night.   Sir William was vigorous and perhaps
ambitious ; with an eye, it seemed to Froude, upon the
Colonial Office at home.   He was so courteous that he had
learned Spanish for the express purpose of paying proper
attention to visitors from the South American continent over
the way.   Froude's neighbour at dinner, the mayor of the
southern township of San Fernando, proved, unluckily, to be
one of those in favour of a free constitution, and bored the
distinguished stranger by eulogising the high characters of
leading personalities in Trinidad.   The company at the long
dinner-table was, however, representative : English, French,
Corsicans and Spaniards, each speaking their several tongues.
The Commodore of the training squadron and some of his
officers were also of the party, their gold braid glinting in the
lamplight.   Conversation during dinner turned chiefly upon
the misdeeds of the President of Venezuela, Guzman Blanco,
and the reviving boundary dispute between his country and
British Guiana.   Later in the evening the guests were entertained by music and Sir William and Lady Robinson sang
Italian duets.   Finally, before the ladies and gentlemen
dispersed to their carriages, to drive round the Savannah now
ablaze with fireflies, the Governor's wife favoured them with

a solo rendering of the *Three Fishers* by Charles Kingsley—
who was looked on, his old friend sourly noted, "as the
personal property of Trinidad : "

> . . . For men must work and women must weep
> And the sooner it's over the sooner to sleep
> And good-bye to the bar and its moaning. . . .

Froude thought Lady Robinson's voice beautiful ; she sang
with real feeling ; and gave to Kingsley's words as much true
meaning " as anyone could do who had no direct acquaintance with an English sea-coast people."

It was almost over.   Cashel sat quietly in a basket chair on
the verandah while the police band played its last piece in the
lamp-lit wood pavilion.   In a chair at his side was a dim
figure clothed in a garment too enveloping to be a tropical
mess-jacket and yet seemingly too white to be anything else :
the archbishop in his soutane, his outlines once more blurred
by the dusk.   It was over till next time : one of the formal,
ordered and pompous dinner-parties for which Cashel was, and
yet was not, rather responsible.   Thirty names had been
selected from the lists.   Thirty names had been scrawled on
scraps of paper and arranged and re-arranged round a card-
board model of the top of the dining room table.   Thirty
names had been printed in gold upon an oblong sheet on
which the top of the same table was represented in royal blue
ink, surmounted by a royal coat of arms.   Thirty persons, the
owners of the names, had assembled in the saloon before
dinner, and had been cajoled by the A.D.C.'s into forming a
wobbly semi-circle in order of precedence.   A trumpet had
been blown.   Their Excellencies had descended the staircase.
They had shaken hands with each guest.   They had headed
the procession to the dining-table, which stood laden with
silver plate and silver branch candlesticks and mounds of stiff
tiger-lilies and little glass saucers of cachou nuts.   The band
had struck up outside the French windows, and as the great
fans whirred on the ceiling, Cashel had peered down the table
and wondered vaguely how it was all going.   There was so

much irrelevant movement that he was always a little bewildered : hands and knives and spoons, turning heads and
active faces, footmen leaning forward with the dishes, the head
butler craning by the door into the kitchens and the pantries;
so many splinters of reflected light—from the gold embroidery
along the captain's sleeves, from the archbishop's amethyst,
from the branch candlesticks, from the cool wine glasses, from
the bracelets of young ladies and the medals of their fathers.
Along the cream-coloured walls of the dining-room King
Edward and Queen Alexandra, King George V and Queen
Mary, imposing, elongated figures in their Coronation robes
stared mildly down on the table from their plaster gilt frames.
When the King's health had been drunk in port and madeira,
and when the ladies had withdrawn, the band retired to the
bandstand overlooking the Savannah and entertained the company until late in the evening. 1939? or 1887? Tradition or
stagnation ? Cashel did not know. " I really must find His
Excellency," said the archbishop, " I fear I must say goodnight."

Froude found many other memories of Charles Kingsley in
Trinidad. In the Botanic Garden behind the new Government House he was shown the straggling wooden building
(now destroyed) which had served as the Governor's Residence
at the time of Kingsley's visit eighteen years before. Unpre-
tentious and rustic, it was called a cottage. It lay at the
" extreme angle " of the Botanic Garden, in a tree-shaded
hollow, separated from the road and the Savannah by clumps
of arched bamboo. Here the room in which Kingsley had
worked was still pointed out, and the gallery up and down
which he would wander, smoking. The Garden itself, which
had given Kingsley so much peasure, was equally delightful
to Froude, who found that it surpassed all descriptions.
Familiar shrubs from English conservatories " were here
expanded into forest giants ; " fronds, fans, creepers, hanging
pods and strange fruits and berries were on every side of him
as he strolled along the winding paths. Each plant seemed
self-consciously surprising : a Portugal laurel produced
blossoms from its stem like a cactus ; an apparently tempting

Mountain Crater, Dominica

Morning Walk, Dominica, 1887

[*From a sketch by Froude*

The Blue Basin, Trinidad, 1887

fruit turned out to be *nux vomica* ; the heavy odour of the manchineel could make the unwary swoon. Some trees had been literally murdered by the " fig vine," which specialised in creeping up the trunks of giant cedars, and strangling the branches ; and then, carried (the gardener said) by a gust of wind, the vine would leap some fifteen feet to the next tree and begin the same performance all over again. In a perfumed glen Froude found the giant nutmegs, with their bright green leaves thinly folded one over the other, and low branches that swept the ground : bowers of greenery proof against tropical rainstorms, and fragrantly attractive to butterflies and moths. Two large butterflies, " the size of English bats," dark blue and peacock green flopped by him as he stood looking at the nutmegs ; he asked a negro boy to catch one for him—the boy refused and " I was penitently glad." Most gorgeous of all the sights in the enchanted garden was the flowering tree of Burma, *Amherstia nobilis*, thick with swinging bunches of vivid crimson blossoms, and making all the spices and oranges, the nutmegs and the cocoa-shrubs look positively drab.

With an obstinacy unusual in visitors to Trinidad, Froude absolutely refused to visit that ugly phenomenon, the Pitch Lake, preferring to spend his days driving to the forests, and gazing at the wonderful trees. Of his various expeditions he reflected later that he had enjoyed the day at the Blue Basin the most. The Blue Basin, a deep pool of water that reflects the azure sky, formed by a cataract and encircled by crags is indeed one of the loveliest sights of the island. Cashel had recognised in it a romantic Highland quality : Walter Scott scenery in tropical terms. You came suddenly upon it (or as Froude put it, " the place broke suddenly " upon you), after a scrambling climb along a narrow overgrown pathway that zigzagged through the forest up a hill. Cashel, who had a supercilious distrust of notorious beauty spots, was amazed by the loneliness and minor grandeur of the scene : the torrent falling over a ledge of rock as it emerged from a tunnel of green branches, and plunging into a deep rippling pool of blue. It seemed very isolated to be so famous ; there were no signs of the tourist ; nor any vestiges of human life at all. The river ran out of the pool as a shallow sparkling stream, with here and there a smaller pool between the jagged bits of rock that lay strewn along its bed.

Froude's journey to the Blue Basin took place by carriage and not by car. They had thus to start earlier than modern visitors and to endure upon the road the almost unendurable heat of noonday, closing the curtains of the carriage to avoid the sun and thus excluding any chance breath of freshening wind. The road itself soon entered the forest and crossed and re-crossed the river, passing groups of huts and negro houses on its way. The mango flowers scented the mid-day air and banana plants waved their flat wide leaves. Upon the ground ripe cocoa-pods were stacked in heaps, like autumn apples in an English orchard. When the end of the carriage road was reached the party descended, handing over their waterproofs and luncheon baskets to some little negro boys who seemed anxious to act as porters to the Basin. And, trudging up the same steep path that one still takes to-day they rounded a buttress of rock and stood confronted with the sixty-foot waterfall and the pool of blue. Along the marges of the pool ferns quivered, and wild plantains, soaked with spray : in clefts above the rocks gnarled and knotted roots of gum trees precariously clung ; while " at the lower end of the pool . . . there grew out from among the rocks near the water's edge tall and exquisitely grouped acacias with crimson flowers for leaves." And, enraptured once more by the fierce crimson tints he had admired in the noble Amherstia, Froude settled down to make a modest sketch of the solitary scene.

Before he left the island Froude was granted an audience with Trinidad's most eminent and remarkable inhabitant, the aged Charles Warner, a member of a distinguished colonial family, who had himself " steered Trinidad through the trying times which followed the abolition of slavery." In Mr. Warner Froude found a man as disillusioned and as gloomy about the Empire's future as himself. The island statesman had but a few more weeks to live ; and his coming death seemed to Froude prefigured in his shrunken stature and pale, intelligent face. It was this, as much as the natural elevation of Charles Warner's character and mind, that impressed Froude as he spoke with him. Listening to this sad " Tory of Tories " foretelling the collapse of the Empire, cursing the " sinister leader " who was ferrying England to her doom, Froude was reminded of Shakespeare's John of Gaunt :

When words are scarce they are seldom spent in vain,
And they breathe truth who breathe their words in pain.

An Empire-builder of the old magnificent race of Empire-builders, Warner perceived the inevitable process of dissolution which Liberalism must bring to the colonies of the Crown. And yet, like Froude, he believed in the British race, and that the day would come, after many decades, when " we should struggle back into sanity again " with the shattered remnants of past greatness and cured for centuries of our illusions. Such harrowing talk, such grim foreboding, was meat and drink to Froude, who felt that to have spoken with such a man was worth a voyage round the globe. One month later Charles Warner lay dead.

Once more on ship-board, speeding back to Barbados by the mail-packet on a wild night, Froude gave some thought to the future prospects of Trinidad. It was clear to him that the English inhabitants would soon be crowded out. The mulattoes and blacks would then quarrel. Trade would drift away to New Orleans and New York. Peace and order would disappear. Obeah worship would increase. Negro felicity would be at an end. And that, he was pretty well convinced, would be that.

In this cheerless state of mind he arrived at Barbados, where the solid parish churches, the officers cantering by on the polo-ground, the smart ladies who rode down the avenues of mahogany with as much elegance as if they had been in Rotten Row, and the thriving cane-fields and sweet potato patches did something to restore his belief in England's civilising power. The training squadron lay out in Carlisle Bay and three American frigates (significant intruders) were jauntily flying the stars and stripes. Froude had, however, already seen Barbados on his way out from England.   He had admired the old Government House and the grotto in its garden, he had wondered why the statue of Nelson in Nelson Square should be painted pea-green, he had noted the incongruous figure of Oliver Cromwell among the monarchs in the stained glass windows of the Assembly Hall, and he had first sampled in Bridgetown the local drink called cocktail.   He was far more anxious now to see Dominica.   The loveliest (they said) and the least known of the Antilles, this island appealed to him also as the scene of Rodney's great fight. And so, after a short stay in Bridgetown, it was towards this little-visited island—one of the Leeward Group and situated between Guadaloupe and Martinique—that he made his way. His ship passed St. Lucia at nightfall, and Froude stood upon the deck to watch the Pitons, those two mist-shrouded peaks of rock, go by in the starlight.   Next morning the ship put in to the chief harbour of St. Lucia for a few hours, negotiating the white coral reefs that glimmered deep down in the blue water. Passing Martinique not long after, they entered the beautiful shelving roadstead of Roseau, the principal and, then, the only, town of Dominica, standing out upon its shallow promontory, the towers of the French Cathedral rising behind a terrace of neat houses, the straight lines of rooftops broken by palm-trees, and to the extreme right the colourless ruins of the old fort.

Set down upon the pier of Roseau by the mailboat, the traveller realised that he had a whole fortnight in which to examine the island that by virtue of Rodney's victory had become the English Salamis.   He knew too that there was no tolerable hotel on Dominica, and so he was doubly gratified to receive a warm invitation from the island's Administrator, Captain Churchill, begging him to stay at the Residency. Two black girl porters snatched his baggage, threw it up on their heads, and marched off through the sizzling heat. Froude followed, wondering apprehensively whether the girls, cracking jokes in their French patois with the native policemen who lounged at the street corners, were laughing at him. Toiling along behind the negresses, up the steep paved path to the Residency, he noticed the cool, pretty English church-

yard, planted with gay exotic flowers. The Residency when
he reached it proved a very respectable kind of a building.
A broad walk with clipped limes along one side, and a lawn
dotted with oleanders and hibiscus on the other, led to the
main door. Lizards basked on the stone steps, and stephanotis shrouded the iron railings with its perfumed blooms.
Captain Churchill and his Creole wife were more than cordial;
and though the Administrator had injured his foot and walked
with a bad limp, he was soon showing Froude over the house,
and down into the garden. From the drawing-room windows
there were splendid views to admire : from one a mountain
gorge covered with forest, from the other a Botanical Garden,
and the Bay fringed with sand and bordered by box-trees and
almonds, and far out to sea an island fortress, captured from
the English by the Marquis de Bouillé in 1778. Captain
Churchill led his guest down into the Botanic Garden for
a fuller inspection. As Froude was gazing at the scene,
which seemed " like a dream," the whole town was suddenly
deluged with heavy rain. Stumbling up again to the Residency
under their umbrellas, they passed a personage who aroused
the stranger's curiosity : a fine-looking French abbé, with a
little white collar and a gold cross. In spite of the rain and
the hurry, the abbé bowed.

This chance encounter called up reflections upon the state
of Dominica under English rule. The island administration
offered many anomalies that invited cynicism : half the
Legislative Assembly was elected by the people and most of
the people who were not black were Europeans of French
extraction : what loyalty could you expect to get from *them* ?
There was a whole hierarchy of revenue officers and hardly
any revenue : there was an inspectorate of roads, but what
roads there were were falling into decay. The soil was some
of the richest in the world, and each year the area under cultivation decreased. Nothing had been done to anglicise this
English colony : and the only powerful Europeans were the
Catholic bishop and his priests and nuns. The chief func-
tionary, Captain Churchill, was powerless and underpaid. In
Dominica Ulysses' bow was indeed unstrung.

As in Trinidad, more of Froude's stay in Dominica was taken up with sight-seeing expeditions than with discussions on island politics. Having decided that Dominica was treated with a ghastly negligence by the Colonial Office, he applied himself to exploring the natural beauties, and to recalling the historical associations, of the country round Roseau. The most notable of his expeditions, and quite on a par with the day at the Blue Basin, consisted of the perilous ascent of the great mountain peak, Mount Diablot, on horseback. The view downwards from the summit—once you had emerged from the clinging dank mists—was very strange ; a panorama of steaming forest, a hidden lake cupped in the crater of an extinct volcano, and bubbling out from all sides the famous boiling streams. When his fortnight was up the mailboat came steaming back to the wharf at Roseau one evening, and, saying goodbye to the kind Churchills by the light of the ship's lanterns, while the whistles shrilled and the few passengers scurried aboard, Froude left Dominica forever : " all that I had seen faded into a memory. . . . But not," he added pointedly, " all that I had thought."

Journeying onward, Froude visited Jamaica, Cuba and Hayti. He sampled the grand, old-fashioned hospitality of Kingston and Newcastle. He stood before the bass-relief that he hoped and believed marked Christopher Columbus' grave. In Havana too he made friends with an invalid American bishop, who was suffering from " clergyman's throat " and had come southward with his Irish chaplain to seek assuagement in the sticky Cuban air. In the streets of Jacmel, in the negro republic, he was struck by the hangdog look the Europeans had. But by the time he reached Cuba it seems as if the novelty and interest of his voyage was wearing thin. His sad mind turned back to the troubles and difficulties he had left behind him in London : and sitting down in the hotel at Havana (so full of noisy, tiresome Yankees) he wrote swiftly and with intense feeling his personal apologia—*My Relations with Carlyle*. This harsh paper, published many years after his death, was his final word upon the hideous and tormenting controversy upon which loyalty and conscience had

first launched him. The confidant of Carlyle's later years·
Froude had relinquished a projected biography of Charles V.
in order to fulfil what he had understood to be Carlyle's dying
wish : the frank publication of the *Reminiscences*, or as they
might better have been termed, the Confessions of Carlyle.
This outspoken volume, together with the works which
Froude himself wrote upon Carlyle, had resulted in a storm of
abuse that had shocked no one so much as the book's editor.
He contended that Carlyle was too fine a figure to justify the
expurgation of his memoirs : that the remorse, the weakness,
the intolerance, the selfishness of the great man were of no
consequence against his essential brilliance and worth. He
saw no possible harm in his own dramatic descriptions of
Mrs. Carlyle's " pale, drawn suffering face." He felt that
the public must have gone mad. Sick to death of the whole
unpleasant business, he had managed to forget it for a time in
the Western Hemisphere. Yet at best he can only have
succeeded in a conscious suppression of his disappointment and
his anger, and there is something fearful in the thought of this
extraordinary old man writing, writing, behind the closed
jalousies of a hot Havana hotel-room, stabbing down upon the
paper the whole sordid truth about the Carlyles' marriage—
his sexual impotence, her bitter frustration—concocting in this
seedy Spanish town a document that has been called " so
poisonous that it should never have been written."

Back in London Froude prepared and published *The English
in the West Indies, or The Bow of Ulysses*. He was quite un-
compromising in his conclusions : everything that could be
done to leave these colonies poverty-stricken and neglected,
to make them sullen and disloyal, had been done by the
Colonial Office : their prospects need not have been, but
indubitably were, quite hopeless. So much for the political
and sociological aspects of his journey. As to natural beauty,
he had seen such sights as he would never forget : the West
Indian islands, he suggested gallantly, were like the novels of
Sir Walter Scott—that seemed the best which you had last
been at.

Chapter Eight

THE LADY OF LAUREL HILL

1825–6

They were hurt at being misunderstood; as philanthropy became intrusive, they began to feel that they were themselves persecuted. They believed that their slaves were happier than English cottagers . . .
WILLIAM CORY *on the West Indian Planters.*

CASHEL FIRST SAW the sugar estates when he went one early morning from Port of Spain to San Fernando, the second town of Trinidad, forty miles to the South. A little railway on an embankment connects the two townships, and from the windows of the narrow carriages he looked down over the cane-fields. It was a swaying, Elysian landscape. Beneath a sky of powder-blue the acres of pale canes trembled in the wind ; scarlet and yellow birds dipped over the pastures : purple butterflies fluttered in the sunshine : at the rural stations stood hedges of pink and cream-coloured flowers like the enamelled toys of Fabergé. Every now and then the train passed a cluster of distant buildings—the white houses of the proprietor, the long negro barracks, the slender chimneys of the usines—that form the heart of each big estate : Coova, Barataria, Valsayn, Orange Grove, La Florissante, Macoya, Santa Rosa, Laurel Hill. As the train leaves Port of Spain it runs beneath the Laventille range, and the high-perched church of Our Lady of Laventille, with squat Fort Picton beside it, is visible for many miles down the line. Soon the island seems to flatten out into a wide cultivated plain, and the big hills crouching round the capital recede until they look like billows of brown smoke. Before it reaches San Fernando the railway runs along the very edge of the sea, the dark waters of the Gulf just beneath the carriage windows, and the Venezuela skyline vague across the way. The journey intoxicated Cashel. Even the huge silver oil-drums, those symbols of modern imperial development, glinted and shone in the sunlight. Returning the same night he found with excitement as the train clanked along the brink of the Gulf, that the black sea-water was streaked with phosphorus. In the moonlight the Caroni swamp and its contorted vegetation looked very sinister : he remembered that bats were said to gather in the branches of the stunted marsh-trees : and, the train coming to a sudden standstill in the centre of the swamp, he listened to the barking of the marsh-frogs. At a wayside station further back along the line a child had thrust a handful of crimson roses in at the carriage door. On either side of the railway track the cane-fields lay smooth and white under the stars.

It is Christmas night in the year 1825. The full moon has mounted high above the cane-fields and the stream that flows through the Laurel Hill pastures, between the noble trees, mirrors its light. At one side of the pasture are the wattled, white-washed cottages of the negroes in a grove of almond trees : at the other the manufactory for sugar and rum. Across the cultivated grounds the thick forest which no one dares to enter is a black shape in this pallid scene. The pasture with the stream lies at the foot of a hill on the summit of which rises the wooden house of the estate owner, Mr. Carmichael, with a giant hog-plum and a Pois-Doux tree beside it. Three-quarters of a mile of untidy lime avenue, grass-grown, and rutted by the wheels of the cane-carts leads to this house. Over the pasture you can see a small river with banana trees upon its banks, and a snow-white cottage for the washerwoman by the water's side. Behind the house towers a hill that is overgrown with brushwood and wild trees : at the hill's top there is said to be a savannah of coarse grass. Down in the negro cottages to-night the Christmas festivities are on. The noise of throbbing drums and voices singing floats up to the house on the hill in the night air. A lady and a gentleman step from the front door into the moonlight, and pick their way down the pasture to the huts. If we follow them the music will become louder : till the lady recognises the old French air of *Le Garçon Volage*. Soon they stand watching eight negro dancers who perform a quadrille in a space of ground encircled by benches and chairs. At one end of this open-air dance floor sit the two drummers, beating their drums: at the other end the piccaninnies of the estate are tripping about in a private dance of their own. The lady gazes round her with approval at the clothes. The ribbons and the artificial flowers which she had bought for them last week at Belmont, and which with the help of the governess she had sewed upon the slaves' dresses certainly look very well. The negro girls are wearing muslin, with coloured sashes, coral necklaces and gilt beads : upon their kid shoes are smart gilded buckles. One negress has a dress of flounced silk, but the older women favour chintz petticoats with a muslin bodice. The old Mammy who is usually in charge of the children's vine gang sports a grand costume decorated with Valenciennes lace. The men are almost all dressed in trousers of grey jean, with embroidered seams and white piping at the pockets. Their jackets and shirts are white and their collars neatly starched. In one of the little huts a well-lit table stands covered with a clean cloth, upon it lines of tumblers and jugs of rum and lemonade and punch and sugared water. There is a solemn silence as the two oldest negroes of the party (the driver and his wife) perform an old-fashioned *pas-de-deux* : but presently they all begin to dance and sing again merrily. They will continue so till morning : the lady and gentleman smile and turn away, walking back up the hill to their house where they will read the evening prayer before retiring to bed.

It was the first Christmas that Mrs. Carmichael, with her husband, her children and Miss F. the governess had spent in Trinidad. A young Scotswoman used to Edinburgh society life, she had first seen the West Indies when as the bride of a St. Vincent planter she landed in that island in December, 1820. Her husband was a widower with children : and Mrs. Carmichael soon found that anyone bent upon doing their duty by their family and their domestics could " find very little opportunity for pleasure in the West Indies." Although society in St. Vincent was not particularly congenial to her, and the meals seemed heavy and long, the dances active and vulgar, she had become fond of the place itself and of her husband's negroes. But when " Mr. C." had decided, about the year 1825, to transfer his family and as many of his negroes as were willing to the fertile island of Trinidad, Mrs. Carmichael was almost as pleased as the slaves. At first sight, too, Trinidad came up to her expectations. The glassy Gulf of Paria reminded her of the print of dear Loch Lomond in Dr. Garnett's *Tour Through Scotland* : when they landed at the quay to be met by Judge Warner's carriage—a smart English equipage with footmen behind—she could hardly believe that she was still in the West Indies. A carriage ! Footmen ! This was indeed a " more polished state of Society " than that over which Sir Charles Brisbane presided in Georgetown, St. Vincent. And as the carriage bowled along through the clean, new town of Port of Spain, with its well-lit shops and the gas-light in the streets, her spirits rose. Belmont, Judge Warner's residence, was an old West Indian house with a fine view from the windows : it looked down over the slight eminence upon which Sir Ralph Woodford's house at St. Anne's was perched. The arrival of Mr. C. and his wife was almost simultaneous with that of Bishop Coleridge and his secretary : and they were as impressed as Henry Coleridge by Sir Ralph Woodford's work. This benign and autocratic governor was at that moment laying out Brunswick Square : he had already planned the road round the Savannah, sponsored the building of a Roman Catholic as well as an Anglican Cathedral, renamed the French streets, and arranged for Mr. David Lockhart, the botanist who had accompanied Tuckey on the celebrated Congo Expedition of 1816, to take charge of a projected Botanic Garden. The standard of English life in Port of Spain was the work of Sir Ralph Woodford, who brought the elements of contemporary English civilisation to this mongrel community. His achievement is suitably commemorated by Lawrence's portrait of him in the Town Hall, and the monument by Chantrey in Holy Trinity Cathedral. Few details escaped the Governor. There exists an inventory in his own handwriting of the cathedral furnishings at Holy Trinity—the prayer-books bound in Russia leather, the Bible for the altar with its golden clasps, the communion table covers of red silk, the damask napkins. On

one occasion he " very strongly urges " the church com-
missioners to send for a proper organist to teach the boys, and
points out that the sooner the choir is made to wear surplices
the better.   On another he gives six bells to the cathedral,
and indicates the days on which in his opinion they should be
rung.   Sir Ralph excelled in other ways than as a man of
taste.   He made friends with the Spanish planters, taking one
of them, Senor Antonio Gomez (the owner of the Pastoria
cocoa-lands which the Coleridges had visited) on a tour of
Scottish country houses.   He gave impartial encouragement
to religion, himself laying the foundation stone of several
Roman Catholic churches in the island.   In every possible
way he tried to assimilate the untidy Latin life of eighteenth-
century Trinidad to the neat commercial habits of an English
colony.   Mrs. Carmichael was immensely struck by the speed
and precision with which he conducted all public business.
" No man ever existed," she wrote, " better qualified for the
government of a colony."

Knowing that she would have no leisure once they had taken
up their residence at Laurel Hill, Mrs. Carmichael set about
sightseeing at once.   During five years in St. Vincent she had
not even managed to find the time to see the Souffriere ;
though her stepdaughter who had made the journey into the
hills had come back with her face skinned by the sun.   Trinidad contains no exciting phenomenon like the Souffriere,
unless you count the dreary pitchlake, with its dingy asphalt
surface pitted by rain-puddles and its circle of scrubby trees.
There are however the famous valleys of Maraval and Diego
Martin.   Mrs. Carmichael was not especially partial to
natural sights : beautiful Maraval seemed not " cool but
absolutely cold," and she shivered beneath its ant-infested
orange trees.   Far more entertaining was a long, hot day spent
in the town with Sir Ralph Woodford and Judge Warner.
Her exile's heart beat faster when she learned that the free-
stone of which the gaol was built had come from her father's
own quarries in Fife : " it was like meeting an old friend."
There were other links with far-off Scotland : Senor Gomez,
who had stayed with the Duke of Atholl and had admired the

beauties of Dunkeld : Mrs. Warner, the judge's wife, whom she had met in Edinburgh years ago. Another day or two was passed in the capital, and then the family set off for Laurel Hill, six miles east of Arima, and began to face up to the spartan comfort and the many duties of life in the wooden house on the hill. Here they found the St. Vincent negroes busily at work side by side with those purchased from the previous owner of the estate. Mr. Warner had been there before them, and left some books which, " added to our own stock made us very independent." The pianoforte was safe after its fourteen-mile journey in a cart, though it needed tuning sadly. The house itself, with its rooms at different levels, and its open rafters in which cockroaches lurked might not seem much to someone fresh from Europe : but it contrasted very well with their home in St. Vincent. Soon Mrs. Carmichael was standing by the door-posts of the new house watching the birds that circled about the Pois Doux tree—the golden Louis d'Or, the gay parrots, an odd bird with light blue plumage, the melancholy, curious Keskadee. But this lively woman had little time for idling. Amongst other tasks she had set herself that of instructing the negro children, and already the picaninies were trotting up the hill for their first lesson. After a little religious teaching she read them a piece of one of Miss Edgeworth's tales, and promised that next time (as a treat) they should be shown a few of Mrs. Trim's Old Testament picture cuts.

Mrs. Carmichael's narrative, published in 1834, and called (perhaps in emulation of Mrs. Trollope) *Domestic Manners of the White, Coloured and Negro Population of the West Indies*, set out unpretentiously to give some facts about West Indian life. Although it appeared at the very height of the Emancipation agitation (in the same year, in fact, that Stanley's hurriedly constructed Emancipation Act was passed) *Domestic Manners* had been written some years before this time, and treated only incidentally of the great problem that was shaking the House of Commons, the Cabinet and the country. The authoress' intention was to portray day-to-day existence on a sugar plantation ; to explain the social condition of the negroes employed upon it ; and to show that for a number of reasons (Emancipation amongst them) sugar-growing was no longer an agreeable nor a profitable occupation. It was her husband's misfortune that he should be trying to run a sugar estate upon model lines at a moment when West Indian sugar had ceased to be king, and the negroes had become surly and truculent through Buxton's reforms. In every way the Carmichaels were ideal colonists. They were humane. They were industrious. They were conscientious. They were religious and civilised. Their complete failure at Laurel Hill was significant of changed conditions. They left the West Indies with the positive conviction that " there seemed no longer any rational prospect of doing good in any sense of the word." " We felt that the really important influence of the proprietor was gone ; that even personal security was in danger ; and in fine that there was no longer any incentive to remain." It is tempting to say firmly that these good people were relics of a past age ; that their conception of the paternal relationship of proprietor to slave was out of date. I suspect that Mrs. Carmichael thought this herself. But we should recall that it was the very rarity of a sense of responsibility and of the practice of virtue in the English planters of the eighteenth century that made these qualities useless in planters of the Carmichaels' day. Mrs. Carmichael believed in slavery, because she thought it involved the protection and instruction of the slaves. In a fertile island like Trinidad the freed slave could earn plenty of money for very little agricultural work ; he became sullen and lazy. Freed negroes no longer wanted the arbitration of the " massa " in their savages' disputes. Even the slave had become disobedient and, at times, offensive. When she asked one of the house-boys for a glass of water there was always the uneasy possibility that he might refuse to bring it. She attributed the planters' difficulties chiefly to the Emancipationists, those ignorant London folk who attended lectures and signed petitions, and had never spent a night in a tropical climate or inspected a sugar refinery in their lives. Resenting the Emancipation movement Mrs. Carmichael began to disbelieve the stories of floggings and tortures of slaves that were agitating educated people in this country. She formed the habit of taking apparently aimless walks through the cane-fields ; she whisked into the sugar manu-factory when least expected : she paid surprise visits to the negro hutments : standing in the shade in her full white dress she watched the lines of workers with their overseers in the fields. This persistent investigation yielded purely negative results. She never saw a flogging, so she supposed they never went on : and most absurd of all to her experienced mind was the English idea that the " driver " (who led the field negroes to labour each day) carried a whip : of course he did not : no driver she had ever seen in St. Vincent or Trinidad carried a whip. Her ignorance on this point is pardonable ; but had she observed other estates, particularly estates in Jamaica and Barbados, with the same keen eye that she applied to Mr. C's utopian lands, she would have seen the long hide thong of the driver, and the bleeding wounds that its cruel and constant application left. It is possible that Mr. Carmichael concealed ugly facts from his mild and inquisitive wife : but more likely that the famous West Indian atrocities were never practised at Laurel Hill at all. It would have been difficult enough to hide anything from Mrs. Carmichael : she wormed informa-tion of the most unlikely kinds out of the unwilling and affectionate " good negroes," and even out of those labelled (by universal consent) " bad negers." During one of her morning walks at Laurel Hill she thought she heard the negro lads singing " rather a singular song." She could not rest until she knew what it was. The house-boy whom she tackled seemed embarrassed, and begged her not to ask about it. " It no good song, missis," he murmured. Mrs. Carmichael had never taken " no " for an answer in her life. She continued to coax and cross-examine, until the poor young negro gave in, and slowly sang the following words to an old Scots air :

Fire in da mountain
Nobody for out him,
Take me daddy's bo tick
And make a monkey out him
    Poor John, nobody for out him.

Go to de king's gaol,
You'll find a doubloon dey ;
Go to de king's gaol,
You'll find a doubloon dey
　　Poor John, nobody for out him.

That was all very well, but what did the song *mean* ? More
embarrassment, more persuasion. At length it was elucidated,
and the mysterious words proved to be part of an insurrection-
ary song. The fire in the mountain was that customarily lit
by negroes intending to burn their master's cane-fields. As
the negroes had lit the fields, nobody would put the fire out.
It was so hopeless that you might as well give the monkeys in
the forests the planter's walking-stick and order them to beat
out the flames. Poor John Bull, nobody would extinguish
the fire that was ruining his crops. While the fire burns, run
to the gaol and seize the money there. It was not a song to
make one feel comfortable at night in one's lonely little wooden
house on an isolated sugar-estate. Perhaps she wished she
had not asked so many questions. And as she sat diligently
copying the verses into her common-place book from memory
she may have sensed how insufficient, how pathetically
inappropriate were Christmas ribands and Maria Edgeworth,
prayer-meetings, or a well-stocked medicine chest to meet the
caustic, malignant hostility of Buxton's negroes. On two
separate evenings she and her husband were warned by the
good negroes that it was dangerous for either of them to leave
the house. It must often have seemed at Laurel Hill that
virtue was indeed its own reward. Justice and kindness sown
in that rich soil gave but a barren yield.

Laurel Hill was a small estate and employed only eighty
negroes (a large estate often had as many as four or five
hundred). It was usual in the islands to put one-third of the
land under cane : the rest of an estate being divided between
pasture, guinea-grass, plantain walks and negro provision
grounds. The sugar year really began in early November
with holing or trenching as a preliminary to planting the canes.
This harsh work (digging all day under a glaring sun in heavy
soil) was allotted to the first or " great gang " of estate negroes

[*After Cazabon*

Village of Arima, Trinidad : in the neighbourhood of the Laurel Hill Estate

[From Waller's " Voyage to the West Indies, 1820 "

A Planter luxuriating in his Hammock

—composed of all the able-bodied men and women. The great gang was also used for road-building, for cutting and carting the sugar-cane and feeding the mill. The holes were filled with manure and light soil by the second gang (elderly men, young mothers, boys from twelve to fourteen years of age). Each month the cane-trenches were weeded, and the cane plants stripped or " trashed." Crop began in February, and the straggling ranks of stooping negroes would move methodically over the cane-fields, slicing the juicy canes with their cutlasses. The boiler-house was then the centre of activity, and it has recently been pointed out that the fundamental mistake of the Emancipationists was their failure to realise that it was this combination of farm-work with factory-work that constituted the real hardship of plantation life. It was as if an English farmer turned manufacturer for half the year. There was no period of respite for slaves or overseer comparable to that of the winter months on an English farm. The only people on a sugar estate who were not badly over-worked were the children of from four to twelve years old. These little negroes were formed into a third gang, called in the case of Laurel Hill, the vine gang, and spent their day wandering up and down the cane pieces under the eye of an old nurse, picking up vines and other bits of greenstuff for the sheep. The aim of the vine gang was to teach the children industry and to get them accustomed to the fields in which the rest of their lives would be spent. Negro children, in Mrs. Carmichael's view, did very well indeed. They were given provision grounds from the earliest age, and by seven years they had plenty of produce to sell. Little boys and girls were given one day a week (besides Sunday) on which to tend their grounds ; and on these days it was noticeable how much earlier they rose, and how much later they worked. Money, recollected Mrs. Carmichael as she eyed them from her hilltop, is the root of all evil : and certainly these little black children (who were given half a crown pocket-money a week) seemed almost mercenary. She felt as she looked at the little creatures hoeing their plots that the negro slave " in youth, maturity or age " was far better off " as regards physical wants " than the peasantry of Midlothian or her own county of Fife. Immediately upon arrival at Laurel Hill Mr. Carmichael had pegged out the provision grounds for each of his negroes. The boundaries at the front and sides of each plot were conspicuously marked, but there was no boundary at the back, and the owner might cut on into the wood for as great a distance as he pleased ; in a year or two most negroes had six acres of their own under thriving cultivation. Their produce was sold, some of it to Mrs. Carmichael, most of it in the country markets at Arima and St. Joseph. To her favourite negroes Mrs. Carmichael used to give handfuls of English cabbage or carrot seed, or a packet of good peas, but the bulk of the slaves' produce consisted of eddoes (for eddoe soup), gourds, pineapples, grapes, alligator pears, sappadilloes, mangoes and mangosteens—for by an old custom the fruit trees of a sugar estate were considered the property of the slaves. Where was the hardship in all this ? Why did not London speech-makers understand these things ? As she gazed at the cane-fields rippling in the wind, the mauve blossoms and the jade-green sheathes quivering in the sunlight, tears of indignation filled her eyes.

A constant source of exasperation on West Indian sugar estates in the eighteen-twenties was the spate of new and sometimes contradictory Orders in Council for the betterment of negro conditions. These Orders in practice annoyed no one so much as the slaves themselves. One Order soon after the Carmichaels had come to Trinidad commanded that all estate negroes should be accurately measured. Mr. Carmichael's efforts to enforce this regulation aroused the terror and fury of the Laurel Hill people, who were convinced that they were being measured for their coffins while still alive. Another Order forbade the immediate flogging of a slave for any offence at all. He was first to be put in the stocks for a set period, and then when his master's anger should have cooled, he might be beaten for his crime. Now, as the Carmichaels were well aware, no negro dreaded the stocks. It was even considered a good way of evading work, for sitting in the shade beneath a mosquito-net, and plentifully fed by one's friends,

St. Vincent's Wharf and the Custom House, Port of Spain

[From a colour-print after Stobwasser

Scene at Grace Bay, Island of Antigua

what did it matter if the ankles and arms could be moved or not ? Some of the new laws amused the negroes immensely, and they would point out that if " massa King George " knew the real facts he would never have sent them a law like that one. As the decade progressed the power of Mr. Buxton seemed to the negroes to increase. Literate slaves could read extracts from his speeches in the news-sheets, and in the end all decided that he was a far superior person in position to King George himself, and quite obviously the head of the English Government. It was clear to Mrs. Carmichael that the authors of the new laws were as well versed in the agriculture and ways of Trinidad as they were in those of the moon.

In spite of its multifarious annoyances, life at Laurel Hill was good. By day there was the work of superintending the house, the kitchens, the negroes, her own children and the governess. She would take the children in a flock for walks along the cane-fences, down the grassy drive between the lime-trees, or even into the wood at the back of the house. Every hour of the day some negro would come running to her : to complain, to excuse, to ask for advice or for medicine, or just to gossip and chatter about other members of their little community. At night there was music and singing to the pianoforte : one had to choose either to keep the windows open and be badly bitten by mosquitoes, or to close the wooden shutters and be suffocated in the heat. European social life in the Trinidad countryside out of easy reach of Port of Spain was almost as exiguous as in St. Vincent. People had little time for courtesy visiting or for cultivating the difficult art of intimate friendship. The months slid by. Torrents of rain beat upon the jalousies, to be quickly followed by long hours of blistering sun. The routine of ploughing and holing and planting and trashing continued with quiet monotony. Crop-time came and went. Christmas was celebrated and then Easter, and then Christmas again. The major excitements of these busy and unprofitable years would be the excavation of a nest of parasol ants from the hillside, or the gathering to seaward of the iron-grey cloud-banks that prelude the hurricane season. Negroes died and were born and were

married.   Mrs. Carmichael transplanted an European shrub
from the neighbouring estate of La Reconnaissance.   Judge
Warner rode over on horseback, and brought her a few new
books.   The governess went shopping in Port of Spain.
A Methodist came and preached to the slaves in her drawing-
room (a much too erudite sermon, well over their woolly heads).
At length it was evident to both husband and wife that they
were really wasting money, energy and time.   They had
better go.   There were only two boats to England before the
end of the summer ; one via New York, the other straight over
the Atlantic to Bristol.   Choosing the second, they began to
pack hurriedly in order to catch it, cutting short their adieus.
The negroes professed the greatest sorrow at their going, but
Mrs. Carmichael could tell exactly which expressions were
genuine and which simulated.   She spent the penultimate day
at Laurel Hill distributing little gifts and remembrances to
their " people."   She walked slowly down her garden and
round the cane-fields for the last time.   On the morning fixed
for their departure, many of the estate negroes gathered round
the house, weeping.   At the bottom of the drive others were
collected, crying and waving their hands.   The carriage jolted
over the cart-ruts and out into the country road.   As it
reached a familiar bend all in the carriage—Mr. Carmichael,
Mrs. Carmichael, the children, the governess—turned round
of one accord and looked back : for each knew that once past
this corner they would be out of sight of Laurel Hill.   For the
last time they gazed silently at the rickety lime-trees in the
avenue, at the funny wooden house in which they had been, on
the whole, so happy, at the cane-fields of which they knew each
fence and pathway, and at the gloomy wood that hid the
savannah upon the top of the further hill.

Landing in England Mrs. Carmichael was a little shocked
by the antics of her creole children.   Although she had taught
them about life in Europe from the books of Mrs. Sherwood,
although she and the governess had striven to instil into them
some sense of what was what, they behaved very oddly indeed
in the Bristol hotel.   They appeared to believe that the bell-
pulls in the bedrooms contained watches, and they went down

on their hands and knees to sniff the white tapestry roses on the embroidered carpets. If this was the result of a good English education in the tropics, what (Mrs. Carmichael wrote almost querulously) could you expect an untutored African to understand ?

The prizes had all been given and the songs were about to begin. In his chair in the front row, Cashel frowned from the stage to his printed programme and back at the stage again. On it were sixteen negro girls in white muslin, with coloured sashes. They stood coyly in two lines. They were going to sing. But what ? And, he muttered to himself, why ? Why should these intelligent and educated young women of Trinidad be made to sing such tunes as *Loch Lomond* and *Allan Water* (these numbers headed the programme) ? They had nothing to do with the Trossachs ; they could have no conception of the scenery upon the banks of Allan Water. Yet, by the same custom that sends tinned mutton, tinned peas and tinned English potatoes to these islands, West Indian youth is fobbed off with tinned Scottish songs. And, he had gathered earlier in the proceedings (when the smiling, bright-faced scholars had stepped up to receive their prizes) with tinned English history too. The boys seemed to have been writing an essay upon the constitutional crises of the reign of Charles the First. Cashel was devoid of any educational theory and ignorant of academic things : but it occurred to him that, unless one classed history-teaching merely as a training for the mind, like mathematics, it might have been as interesting to teach these young negroes some West Indian history instead. And then these songs. He wondered what would happen if he got up and suggested that they should sing " Fire in de mountains." He imagined a letter to the Principal : " this delightful old song which brings back to us the early days of British rule in Trinidad, and illustrates so well the contemporary relationship between the communities." But the girls were already declaiming that they and their true loves would never meet again on the bonny, bonny banks of Loch Lomond. It was sickening.

The relationship between the communities . . . Cashel had not been long enough in Trinidad to formulate any opinion on it at all.   A few weeks in a place may give you an accurate impression of the atmosphere, the tone : it cannot provide you with a sound basis for a political or sociological point of view. As a matter of fact he never came to any conclusion about this delicate problem : he got no further than noticing certain aspects of island society, certain factors which would have contributed to any judgment he might have decided to make. To begin with, it was fairly evident that the official attitude that there was no difference between black and white, coloured and European was as fallacious in its essence (but not in its practice) as the social one that there was all the difference in the world.   Undoubtedly there were differences. He often observed, for instance, that when he found someone who seemed to him particularly lively or interesting or clever, he was pretty certain to be told later that that person had coloured blood.   At such times he recollected Trollope's prophecy about the coloured races : how they would combine African vitality with European brilliance.   He also noticed a difference in topics of conversation.   Educated people of African origin would speak to him of subjects about which he was accustomed to talk in his own country : about books, music or religion.   English persons on the other hand, spoke mainly of tennis-scores, the country-club, whiskey or precedence or oil or (if they were officials) reminisced with anecdotes of high-jinks at the Raffles Hotel, Singapore.   Cashel was not con-ceited enough to think the topics he preferred superior to the others : it was only that they were the topics he preferred. In spite of the habits of politeness, almost of caution, that governed white relations with persons of darker hue, he began to classify his white acquaintances.   There was the first category of personages whom he could only call to himself " aggressively white."   The aggressive whites struck him as foolish.   They missed so much fun.   They were perfectly capable of putting themselves into Coventry for a whole evening, because their neighbour at dinner happened to have a drop, a taint of coloured blood.   They did not seem to behave with similar reserve towards members of the Indian community in the island. It was all very hard to understand. Another category regarded negroes as charming and picturesque children, but children that were difficult if spoilt. Another category was made up of persons themselves tinged with the blood of Africa : and at pains to conceal a self-evident affinity. There were several more classes but Cashel, with his ignorance and inexperience, saw no reason to trust his own judgment. Many of the little indications he noticed may well, he used to feel, have been utterly imaginary. Occasionally these indications were of such a nature that he most passionately hoped that they were indeed inventions of his own brain.

Chapter Nine

THE DUCHESS OF ALBEMARLE'S PHYSICIAN

1687

> He hangs in shades the orange bright,
> Like golden lamps in a green night,
> And does in the pomegranates close
> Jewels more rich than Ormus shows.
> ANDREW MARVELL : *Bermudas*

IT WAS COOL in the Assembly Rooms, after the beach.

As the Attorney talked on affably in his soft Barbadian drawl, Cashel looked around. He found it much as he had imagined : a legal-looking chamber with a vaulted roof, furniture in dark leather, wainscoting in dark wood, a horseshoe of dark seats for the deputies. The blinding light of midday, that blazed in Nelson Square outside the windows, was filtered here through lunettes of painted glass, containing the portraits of our English sovereigns since James the First. The windows serve to remind visitors of the age and dignity of the colony of Barbados, and of its long connection with the Crown.

" You'll be blown away in Barbados," they had said on the boat, " and be given flying fish to eat." The wind in fact had not seemed to Cashel very noticeable so far ; and he had been given mutton for lunch. In Bridgetown there was the usual glare of tropical daylight ; the usual clusters of cerise blossoms hanging over white garden-walls ; piles of unripe bananas in the warehouses ; young negresses balancing baskets on their heads ; ships' masts seen over tiled roof-tops ; earthenware pots and pans for sale on the quays. In front of this low, white port lay Carlisle Bay, a flawless arc of shining water, thinly green. Bathing that morning from the Club beach he had been fascinated by the foreshortening of human limbs in the translucent water. Far out in the bay white sails gleamed and darted. The white sand of the beach was strewn with prickly objects—nuts ? fruits ? catkins ?—that had evidently been discarded by the trees. Scattered about upon the sand, too, were some thick flat leaves and some pretty sea-shells. His feet hurt him where he had burned them on the tarmac outside the bathing-hut, after taking off his clothes. But cold rum punch sitting on a bench in the shade had been delicious, and after luncheon somebody had played on the piano, and the notes had gone twanging through the high empty rooms and passages, and up and down the staircases of Government House, and out into the garden where parasite creepers hung stilly in the heat.

The Attorney-General was now discussing the riots of 1876. Cashel stopped looking at the lunettes. He asked about the Governor then, Governor Pope-Hennessy, who was said to have sympathised with the negroes.

" Oh, the Governor," said the Attorney-General, " we didn't like him so we sent him home."

" Really," said Cashel. He looked up at the lunettes again. Besides the wind and the flying-fish he had been warned against Barbadian arrogance. His eye travelled from the head of James the First to that of James the Second. A community that had so staunchly supported the Stuart cause would not, he supposed, have much use for a liberal tradition. But it was too hot outside and too cool in here to do much consecutive thinking. The contrast made him feel rather faint. His feet still hurt from the beach. The sweat in which his shirt was drenched was clammy. The lunette windows seemed to grow clearer and larger. The royal faces wobbled and flickered before his eyes. He fixed his gaze on James the Second, in a heavy peruke. He was no longer listening to what the Attorney-General said.

Heralded by a flock of sea-birds, the *Assistance* frigate sailed into Carlisle Bay. From her tall topmast an admiral's pennon fluttered, and as the ship, followed by its satellite yacht and merchantmen, entered the bay all the guns along the forts of Bridgetown and in the vessels that lay anchored in the still harbour thudded in a dull salute. On the deck of the frigate the Duchess of Albemarle and her ladies peered curiously at this low island and its leaning palm-trees. On the quay of Bridgetown the Governor of Barbados, Sir Edwin Steel, waited anxiously for the passengers to land. For here (at last) was the Governor-designate of Jamaica, the young Duke of Albemarle, a personage of singular lustre in the last reign and for all Barbadians knew of equal influence under the present monarch. In any case, the Duke, a great political figure and the direct representative of King James the Second, came fresh from the galleries of Whitehall Palace and the life of power and elegance that now radiated once again from such houses as his wife's ancestral home at Welbeck Abbey. Cheered by the crew of the *Assistance*, the Duke and Duchess stepped ashore to be ceremoniously received by Sir Edwin Steel. Soon they were dining with the island notables, and tasting shaddocks and guavas and pines and mangrove grapes and " all other unknown fruits in Europe " to their amazement and delight. But the joy of arriving at Barbados was damped by some heavy storms of rain ; and the sharp and sudden ill-ness of the Duke of Albemarle cast a thin shadow of apprehension and gloom.

The Duke and Duchess, who had set off from England to the sound of Plymouth's guns, had been eight weeks on the way. Their only sight of land had been Madeira, where they had stopped just long enough to visit some convents and take on board more wine. For many days these Lelyesque persons had suffered from the *mal de mer* : and when they had recov-ered from this indisposition, and had discussed analytically with their physician the causes of sea-sickness and the nature of green bile, they began to feel the heat. As the ship neared the Equator, the tallow-candles drooped in their gilded sockets ; the butter melted ; the travellers sweated horribly and their skin burst out into pimples and spots. It was no comfort to be told by Dr. Sloane that these eruptions were the " greatest advantage they could have," nor that " sunbeams were too spiritual to be poisonous." Bleeding and purging were the order of the day on board the *Assistance* ; and soon Doctor Sloane was able to prove to his own satisfaction that lice do not " as some ingenious men think die south of the tropic." Flying-fish flopped on to the decks. Noddy birds rocked

solemnly in the rigging. A sea-snail floated by ; so did a
jellyfish or " sea-nettle " (which the travellers concluded to be
a " middle nature between a Plant and an Animal ") ; on the
fifth of November they were greeted by the famous Tropic
Bird ; a shark was caught by the sailors and was found to have
inside its head an " unctuous, viscid, slippery and mucilagi-
nous " liquid. But in spite of all these delightful novelties
the sumptuous temporary cabins erected in the frigate for the
Duchess and her attendants remained hot, stuffy and unpleasant. Only a small fraction of the paraphernalia of rich
aristocratic life could be crammed into a frigate carrying forty-
four guns. All the same, they were travelling in state.
Their retinue of one hundred servants were chiefly accommo-
dated in the yacht. Their food, wine and baggage (the latter
weighing five hundred tons) were divided up between the yacht
and the two merchantmen. The baggage included such
diverse articles as the Duke's gold dressing-plate, and enough
copies of the Thirty-Nine Articles to go round all the churches
of Jamaica : the complete furniture of a chapel, some books of
homilies and fifty-two tons of beer. There were also some
boxes of stiff parchment—grants, patents and commissions
that in effect authorised the Duke of Albemarle to make as
much money for himself and the King out of the West Indies
as he possibly could.

To those unaware of the patents stowed away in the
Assistance's hold, the Duke of Albemarle's decision to accept an
appointment in remote Jamaica came as a shock and a surprise.
People who did not know the Duke may have supposed
patriotism was his only motive, and it seems that we should
count amongst these *ingènus* the worldly-wise poetess, Afra
Behn. Mrs. Behn professed (in a Pindaric) to believe that
the Duke :

> . . . now for Fame ignoble ease disdains,
> Bravely resolv'd, he breaks the Lazy Chains . . .
> A Prince whom no Ignoble Interest sways
> To trust his fortune to the fickle seas.

A Privy Councillor, a Knight of the Garter, Chancellor of
Cambridge University, Lord Lieutenant of three counties,

Colonel of the King's Own Regiment of Foot, the Duke
seemed too omnipotent and indispensable a figure for even a
temporary colonial exile. But the prime motive for the
voyage was a financial one. In 1687 the Duke of Albemarle
was thirty-four : from his father, old George Monck, he had
inherited a dukedom, an impressive fortune, and the favour
of King Charles. Through his wife Elizabeth Cavendish,
eldest daughter of Lord Ogle, the son and heir of the Duke of
Newcastle, he could claim a connection with half the great
families of England. When his father died in 1670 Christopher Monck was just seventeen and newly married: and for
the next decade his career is a tale of accumulating honours and
of ostentatious magnificence. The wealth carefully amassed
by George Monck and his wife Anne Clarges was spent in a
careless but princely manner by their son : the huge, ill-fated
mansion of New Hall in Essex was bought and furnished : in
London the Albemarles kept spectacular state at their house
in Piccadilly, employing Verrio to paint their ceilings, and
maintaining several carriages, and a state river-barge. By
1682 their means had dwindled, and selling Albemarle House
they were fain to accept with pleasure the loan of the old Duke
of Newcastle's unfashionable town residence in Clerkenwell.
Although in 1684 the Duke made nearly forty thousand
pounds from his shares in the famous salvage venture of the
day—the Great Plate Wreck that lay off Hispaniola, and
yielded doubloons encrusted with coral and bars of seaweed-
covered gold—this windfall did not suffice ; and when, after
raising the Devon and Cornwall militia to fight Monmouth's
rebellion in 1685, Albemarle was appointed Governor of
Jamaica, we may imagine that the prospect was welcome to
him. Financially, he should gain much by exploiting the
West Indian Islands as his patents permitted him to do, and
there was the possibility of getting more gold raised from the
Hispaniola wreck. Politically it could do him no harm to
leave England at this particular time. The Court was turning
Catholic, and uncertain of his own position with the new
King, he dallied on in England month after month, but at
length in September 1687 he set sail ; a portly, red-com-

plexioned nobleman, made unhealthy by drink and court life and " sitting up late and often." He was, as it proved, leaving England for good.

The Duchess, who was only one year younger, is a different and less conventional character. She was the granddaughter of that ornate authoress, Margaret Duchess of Newcastle. Probably she had inherited some of her grandmother's startling eccentricities, for though strictly brought up by Lady Ogle (" those liberties others think very reasonable are not thought so by us ") she had turned out spoiled, strong-willed and frivolous, devoted to power and position, a trifle mad. To-day she might have got away with it by being called " highly-strung " or neurotic ; but to the seventeenth century her fits of anxiety and melancholy and her bursts of temper were infallible signs of madness. Her experiences in Jamaica increased her mental disorder, and for the last forty years of her existence she was kept shut up by her family, living proudly in the insane belief that she had married *en seconde noces* the Emperor of China, a sad, squalid conclusion to a life begun with gaiety and elegance. An early portrait at Welbeck shows her seated, in stiff silken draperies, with pearls round her throat and twined in her hair. She has a long face of peculiar distinction and beauty, light chestnut-coloured ringlets to her shoulders, and slanting eyes. But her expression is excessively disdainful, and it is easy to divine that stubborn passion for wealth and grandeur that made her chivvy her ailing husband unceasingly to alter yet further in her favour his already generous will. By her letters she seems warm-hearted: " We are just parting from England," she writes her sister Lady Margaret Cavendish on the 10th of September 1687 from Portsmouth, " Pray dear give my affection to sister Bell. God bless her." But though calm and sensible at the time of her departure from England, she had already showed symptoms of insanity, and had been at various periods under the care of an old physician, Dr. Peter Barwick. Dr. Barwick treated her with all the tolerance of a modern psychiatrist, suggesting to members of her family draft letters that they should write to ease her mind. It was through Doctor

Barwick that a young London physician of twenty-seven was engaged to go to Jamaica with the Duke and Duchess at a salary of six hundred pounds a year. His name was Dr. Sloane.

Hans Sloane forms the focus of interest in this strange Jamaican adventure. From the point of view of everyone else who took part in it, the voyage was an unmitigated failure. It killed the Duke. It made the Duchess more insane. It exacerbated the islanders of Jamaica. It set local officials at loggerheads and confounded the colonial lords at home. It meant that several persons in the Albemarles' household were on the wrong side of the ocean at the time of William III's invasion of England, and thus missed the opportunity of turning their coats. For all these the expedition was more than a waste of time, it was definitely unfortunate : but Doctor Sloane, earnest, professional, inquisitive, used every moment of his twelve months in the tropics to brilliant advantage. When he finally returned to England with the Duchess and the Duke's embalmed corpse, he brought with him cabinets of dried plants, of shells and corals and snakes, animals and birds that became in the next century the nucleus of the British Natural History Museum. He brought with him too in his note-books a quantity of novel information that added most effectively to the scientific knowledge of Europe in his own day. During the reign of Queen Anne he industriously compiled from his note-books two monumental quarto volumes, entitled *A Voyage to the Islands*. When this lavish expedition was finished, when the last gun had boomed a salute, and the last banquet was over, when the admiral's pennon was folded and the gilded temporary cabins fallen to dust, what was left ? What remained from so much pomp and flourish, intrigue and sycophancy, excitement and expense? Something concrete and permanent : a small addition to human knowledge of the laws of the universe : a few new facts unearthed in a tropical island by this tall, pallid young man who possessed a disinterested purpose that his fellow-travellers lacked.

[From the portrait by Slaughter in the National Portrait Gallery

Sir Hans Sloane in 1736 (aet. 65)

Elizth Cavendishe 3st
Daughter to Henry Duke
of Newcastle Married to
Christopher Monk 2^d
Duke of Albemarle

[From the portrait by Lely at Welbeck Abbey

Elizabeth Cavendish, Duchess of Albemarle

" This is indeed a world of new things.   You may be sure
the task I have is already delightful to me."   Dr. Sloane was
writing to his friend Robert Courten soon after they had
landed in Barbados.   Already the sight of wild geese and
New England deer had stirred him, and when he tasted the
exotic dessert served at their first banquet on shore he felt
" all my fatigues well-bestowed when I came to have such
a pleasant prospect."   His comments on the phenomena seen
during the voyage are an odd mixture of the medieval with the
modern.   He was ready to attribute fabulous powers—the
smell of the sea-spurge " cures hysteric fits "—to some
objects, while showing great common sense over others.   His
most admirable trait was his ruthless anxiety to analyse and to
compare.   He insisted on getting examples of everything he
saw at sea, trying his best to find affinities between new
phenomena and those about which he had read at home.
One of the things that gave him most trouble was the phosphorus at the ship's sides.   What was the *nature* of this
mysterious light ?   Nicolas Papin had called it *mer lumineuse* ;
others compared it to a lanthorn or to diamonds.   Was it not
perhaps decaying fish-matter ?   The only answer was to get
some of it into his hands.   But how hard this was.   " I
endeavoured with a swab several times dipt into the Water to
pull some of those Sparkles up, but could not, for they would
not stick to it."   In the end he got a bucket from a sailor and
let it down into the Atlantic : the sparkles were caught.
Doctor Sloane described everything he saw with minute
precision : grampuses, porpoises, dolphins, sea-feathers,
booby-birds, although throughout the voyage he was kept
extremely busy with the ailments of his employers, their
attendants and the crew.   Never, indeed, during his year in
the tropics did he let his scientific curiosity run away with him :
never was his enthusiasm permitted to interfere with the
arduous routine of professional duty as chief physician to the
Duke's Fleet.   In Jamaica itself he had to combine his tiring
journeys to get plants in the interior of the island with the
daily doctoring not only of the Duke and Duchess and their
household but of the rich planters and the wretched slaves as

well.   He was stern and impartial : ordering cupping, bleeding, purging and his great stand-by, the Steel Course, with the
confidence of authority.

After ten days of jollity at Barbados (during which the Duke
reviewed the troops, fell ill, and learned to his chagrin that the
only mineral in the Island was marcasite ; while his doctor
botanised happily, collecting roots and stalks, seeds and pods)
the whole party embarked once more and set off up the
islands.   The Pitons of St. Lucia; the lone volcano of Martinique; Dominica and Guadaloupe shrouded in forests; pyramidal
Redonda passed before their wondering eyes.   The last
struck Dr. Sloane as hideously barren, but he was assured that
it contained at least some acres of fertile ground and was the
haunt of " Boobies and other Birds that come hither to lay
their Eggs at proper Seasons."   The population of Nevis, two
thousand of them, assembled for an inspection by the Duke.
But what a population !   " Swarthy," noted Doctor Sloane
and " of a yellowish sickly look."   On climbing a hill in Nevis
to pick flowers he was angered to find a sharp and private
rainstorm in progress at the top of it, for he had yet to learn
about the weather in the West Indies.   From Nevis they
proceeded to St. Kitts, where the Governor showed them
Brimstone Hill.   Passing St. Eustatius and Porto Rico they
entered, on the nineteenth of December, the secure and
sheltered harbour of Port Royal.   Their outward journey was
ended.   They stepped ashore in Jamaica to find a three-day
public entertainment prepared for them by the officials of the
island, who were hoping against hope that their new Governor
would prove to be a courtly nonentity.   The Duchess was not
forgotten in the welcome, and we may picture her listening
coolly to the extravagant praises of the public speeches.   In
one of these orations she was assured that her presence in
Jamaica was " an honour which the opulent kingdoms of Peru
and Mexico would never arrive at " and that Columbus' ghost
would rest appeased could he but know " such hallowed footsteps " had trod his island soil.

In 1687 the English were comfortably established in
Jamaica.   Port Royal already exhibited many of the charac-

teristics, and some of the mistakes, that mark English life in the colonies. Doctor Sloane at once observed that Spanish houses were made of clay and reeds, with tiles or palmeto thatch ; these houses were low and cool. " The houses built by the English," he writes, " are for the most part brick and after the English manner . . . are neither cool nor able to endure the shocks of Earthquakes." Europeans in Jamaica obstinately wore the clothes they were accustomed to in England : the wise negroes wore nothing but a " little canvas jacket and breeches . . . given them at Christmas." Outside Port Royal, in the country, the planters' houses stood remote alike from the noisy smelly sugar works and from the oblong huts of the negroes. These negro huts Doctor Sloane found scantly furnished : a mat for sleeping, an earth pot for cooking yams, some hollowed calabashes for cups and spoons. The blacks, he reflected, were " a very perverse generation of people," and yet even so the punishments for bad slaves seemed excessive—whipping till they bled, and then the deliberate application of hot wax or cayenne pepper to the open wounds. The slave trade, organised by the Royal African Company, of which the King was Governor, was a busy concern. The Company's factor, Colonel Molesworth, had acted as Lieutenant Governor of Jamaica for the last three years. As supervisor of the monopoly rights of London shareholders he was hated by the planters. Albemarle was no stranger to the embittered politics of Jamaica, for, a Lord of Trade and Plantations at home, he had seen the distant repercussions of these controversies. Now, as Governor, he determined to intervene in them. Backing the planters he sent Molesworth in disgrace to London, where the factor spread tales of the Duke's misgovernment that ultimately reached the Court. Though Albemarle was an unwise Governor he was never an unprincipled one. With his patents and commissions, his bond to give the King one-fifth of further treasure from the Plate Wreck, one-half of the yield of any new wreck that might be raised, he could not be disinterested : but he tried to suppress piracy, and to appoint persons of ability to suitable positions in the island. A true

8

viceroy of the Stuarts, he dissolved the House of Assembly when a member quoted *Salus Populi Suprema Lex* and the erudite deputy was arrested, and fined six hundred pounds. The elections for the new house were carefully supervised, and the resulting Assembly, a menial but sullen body, was unpleasantly reminiscent of the last House of Commons in the reign of Charles the Second.   We can say safely that Albemarle's rule pleased no one in the island, yet we should remember the multitude of upright English Governors in the West Indies of whom the same has been true.   But political squabbles did not interfere with prosperity, and already Jamaica was a wealthy island.   Trade was carried on clandestinely with the Spaniards, and with the Dutch at Curaçao ; openly with New England and New York.   The main exports to Europe were sugar, ginger, indigo, cotton-wool, cachao nuts and sarsparilla ; imports from home were beef, pork, biscuits, liquor and clothes.   The standard of life, however, was not as high as in England, and the Duke and Duchess disdainfully rejected two houses outside Port Royal prepared for their reception, ultimately renting one from the Deputy-Governor at an exorbitant price.

Not long after landing Doctor Sloane was taken ill.   To him it seemed a dangerous fever, but to local people it was just " a little seasoning."   In January the fever attacked him again and swept on through the Duke's household—headaches, " vomiting to no purpose " and other symptoms. Attributing it to colds caught when the sheets fell off at night, Sloane prescribed a twelve-ounce bleeding, with blistering for the delirious, and a strict regimen of lemon juice and barley water.   Cold treatment was obviously called for ; hot treatment would be fatal.   His fame as a doctor fresh from London spread throughout the island.   Planters, their wives, children, servants and slaves took to calling at the Spanish two-storeyed wooden house in which he lived.   Here, in a room filled with cabinets, with an aviary outside the window, he examined all classes and colours with a just impartiality, ordering the prescriptions he had applied to the ducal household on the *Assistance*—bleeding, purging, cupping, blistering, mint Julep,

Locatelli's Balsam, Hartshorne, the Steel Course.   Of most of
the cases he kept records, and nasty reading they make—
gangrenes, swellings, putrefactions, vomits, rashes and boils.
Many of the Europeans' ailments were due to over-indulgence,
mostly in drink.   A noted drinker, Sir H. M., " aged about
45, lean, sallow-coloured, his Eyes a little yellowish and Belly
prominent " complained of lack of appetite from drink.
Dr. Cooper, who was fond of rum punch, found that this
favourite potation now gave him violent pains.   Mrs. L.
drank too much wine and fell into a Cholera Morbus, from
which Doctor Sloane revived her with thin chicken broth.
Mr. Lane protracted his bout of fever by " privately drinking
white Madeira wine contrary to direction."   Mrs. Fuller
had a swimming in the head, and was tormented by Incoherent
Fancies at nightfall.   A youth of twenty-four took part in a
drinking match and paid for it by falling into a fit.   It is easy
to laugh at this catalogue of folly ; but it is probable that the
prevalence of drunkenness amongst the Europeans and white
creoles was directly due to the frustration and discomfort of
seventeenth century colonial life.   The negroes—turners,
tailors, joiners, drivers, wheelwrights, footmen—who came
streaming in from remote plantations had their own ailments.
Sometimes these negro disorders were purely psychological, as
in the case of Rose, a children's nurse, who had grown suddenly
" Melancholy, Morose, Taciturn and by degrees fell into a
perfect Mopishness."   The slaves were up to all sorts of
tricks to obtain medicine, sympathy and attention : and some
of Doctor Sloane's pages might have been written one hundred
and fifty years later by Mrs. Carmichael or Waller.

In the preface to his second volume of the *Voyage to the
Islands*, published twenty years after the first, Sloane is at
pains to point out that the many hundreds of plates which it
contains, though drawn by people who had never seen the
living trees and flowers, are perfectly accurate.   Each plate,
copied from a dried specimen in his museum at Chelsea, had
been checked by him personally before it was engraved.
Errors might seem inevitable ; but he flattered himself that
they had been practically eliminated.   The Jamaican collec-

tions, which formed a sensational part of his Museum, consisted chiefly of eight hundred specimens of plant life. Of
some of these he possessed duplicates, which he gave away to
distinguished foreigners ; sending at one time sixty species of
ferns to Paris, a piece of generosity that goaded the French
savants into financing an expedition across the Atlantic to prove
that Frenchmen could find even more. How did he form his
collections ? How find the time to pluck, press and preserve
so many rare specimens, amidst the importunities of his doctoring life ? Sometimes he would go off on horseback with a few
local gentlemen, a draughtsman and a guide, intent on reaching the north shores of the island, through the forests and the
hills. Sometimes he would set off alone, before daybreak, as
the sun dissolved the mists before the Saltpans. He always
carried a billhook with him, to hack at shrubs and guinea-
grass, and to lop branches off some unnamed tree. On some
days he would wander along the beach, gathering shells and
corals, seaweed and sea-spurge. Others again were devoted
to the interior of the island : and we may picture him, in his
broad-brimmed hat, as he cuts his way through the woods.
Every now and then he reaches upwards to sweep aside a
parasite creeper or pick a leaf from some emerald tree. More
often he stoops amongst the spiky grasses to gouge up a new
root, or cut the stalk of a speckled yellow or crimson flower.
Occasionally his investigations continued so late that he was
benighted in the forest ; when he would lie down to sleep on
a pallet of palm leaves, in some dank wayside hut " interrupted
by the Croaking of a sort of Tree Frogs." We can see him
moving beneath the meeting branches of trees with grey and
silver trunks ; moving warily with the eagerness of the pioneer
and the expert, thrusting away the coiling foliage, trampling
through the rotting leaf-mould. Free of the woods, he comes
out upon the Maggotty Savannah, where close to the ground
grows a " small and low sensible Plant " on which you can
write your name with a switch, the forms of the letters remain-
ing legible for some time. Back once more in his room he sits
up late at night over his Cabinets, ticketing and comparing the
day's prizes, searching his Latin dictionary for a suitable new

name for each discovery. It was a perfect twelvemonth. He
was happy with the full ripe happiness that is brought only by
true vocational fulfilment.

In his contract as physician to the Duke and Duchess of
Albemarle, Sloane had stipulated that, should the Duke and
his " fleet " be called back to England, he himself could stay
on in Jamaica if he wished. The death of the Duke in
October 1688 sent the doctor's plans awry. He could not
leave the crazy Duchess, that " Disconsolate Princess " as the
Assembly called her, to face the voyage to England alone.
Even in Jamaica she was threatened by perils, for the very
grandeur of the state she and her husband had kept made her
person and her gold and jewelry a tempting object for any
of the local buccaneeers. Doctor Sloane embalmed the Duke's
body, while the Duchess withdrew to a house in the country
where, guarded day and night by the militia, she waited for a
ship to England. In London, meanwhile, the reign of James
the Second was at its end. At Christmas, which the Duchess
spent with her ladies at Guanaboa, the Stuart King was in
France. Rumours of English events reached Port Royal
during the winter. The anxiety of the Duchess increased.
Until the death of the Duke she seems to have remained calm
while in Jamaica, but then we get few glimpses of her during
1688, and none that really indicate her state of mind. She
wrote letters from time to time to her friends in England ;
short letters, they complained, that told them nothing of what
was then called " how like." They were mainly notes of a
diplomatic character ; her compliments to Lady Sunderland,
her duty to the Queen. She sent tropical fruit to Mary of
Modena, and a packet of chocolate to drink which did not
arrive. " As to the jacolet, it is not to be heard of," wrote one
lady in waiting to her " dearest Duchess : " " since your
Grace was so obliging as to say you sent me some jacolet "
wrote another, " I will tell you the truth, that I never had it
. . . I wish I could find out by what hand it was sent, because
I have told the Queen of it." The long, misspelt epistles
which she got in return for her short notes kept her in touch
with the salient outlines of the social scene : the Duchess of

Monmouth's marriage, Lord Mordaunt's attempt to find a Plate Wreck, the Duchess of Portsmouth's return to England, the Queen Dowager's cancellation of her Lisbon voyage. At court the news of the Duke's death caused a few jocular speculations about his will, but that was all. One of King James' last acts was to reverse everything Albemarle had done in Jamaica, to knight Colonel Molesworth and to order him back to the island as Governor.

The Duchess and her suite, her jewelry and her plate were embarked at last on March 16th, 1689. For four days they sailed along the Jamaican coast. On the fifth they put off into the ocean, and by the 26th March they were well away into the Sargasso Sea. On the 17th of April the Duchess changed ships in mid-Atlantic, going first from the *Assistance* to the Duke's yacht, and then to a well-defended frigate. With her went her husband's leaden coffin, her ladies and her footmen ; Doctor Sloane, his cabinets and a yet more precious cargo : his living animals. "Though I foresaw the Difficulties, yet I had an Intention to try to bring with me from Jamaica some uncommon Creatures alive." These comprised a large yellow snake, seven foot long; a Guana lizard; an alligator ; and some other reptiles. The first casualty was the snake. It had been put by Doctor Sloane into a large earthen jar covered with boards, and fed on fowl-guts and garbage. "Weary of its confinement, it shoved asunder the two Boards," wriggled on to the roof of a cabin occupied by the Duchess' footmen, "who being afraid to lie down in such Company shot my Snake dead." It was particularly unfortunate, as the snake had seemed to like its new home, which was infested by rats—"the most pleasing food for these sort of Serpents." The Guana lizard was loose and lived comfortably on calabash-pulp, till one day, running along the gunwale of the yacht, it was frightened by a seaman and jumped overboard. The alligator died a natural death in its tub of saltwater on the forecastle, in the middle of May. It was immediately dissected by the doctor, who found its ribs crooked and cartilaginous and that the intestines were wound " in many fine Circumvolutions." None of the living animals

[*From Stedman's " Voyage," 1796*]

Monkeys of Guiana

[*Ackermann lithograph after Caddy*

Town and Harbour of Kingstown, St. Vincent, in 1837

survived : " and so it happens to most People, who lose their strange live Animals for want of proper Air, Food or Shelter," was his sad comment. On May 28th the water through which they sailed seemed shallow and very greenish. It was filled with fine sea-shrubs like those that Doctor Sloane had seen long ago in London, one of which had been kept by Charles the Second in his Closet for many years before his death. On the next day they sighted the Scillies and soon they were nearing Plymouth. But, travellers from a remote, exotic world, they were ignorant of the current news in England. Was there Peace or War ? If they went up the Channel would they be taken as a prize ? The Duchess had transferred from the *Assistance* because she was afraid the Master was going to carry her, an unwilling follower of King James, into a French port. It would be idiotic to be captured now in an English one. The Channel water was covered with floating chests and casks heaved overboard from English ships; in preparation, the apprehensive exiles presumed, for a sea-fight. Doctor Sloane was despatched in an armed boat to reconnoitre the approaches to Plymouth Sound. They came up with a fishing boat, and he asked it where the King was. " Which King ? " replied the fisherman : " King William is well at Whitehall, King James is in France." War was on ; the Channel was full of Privateers ; many prizes were being seized. The doctor was rowed back to the Jamaica flotilla and imparted this news. The ships came quietly into Plymouth the same day, and " soon after, her Grace the Duchess of Albemarle Landed with most of us, her Plate, Jewels, etc., and came up, thanks be to God, with Safety by Land to London." This nervous, secretive homecoming contrasted sharply with the showy departure from England eighteen months before. Fate and Death had played havoc with the Albemarles' ambitions. But no change of monarch, no shift of politics could take from Doctor Sloane the profits he alone had derived from this Voyage to the Islands : his cabinets of fern leaves which he bequeathed to the nation, his knowledge which he published to the world.

Chapter Ten

AT LAST

1869

At last the dream of forty years, please God, would be
fulfilled and I should see the West Indies. . . .

CHARLES KINGSLEY

As soon as they reached the rest-house they began to fry eggs
for breakfast. It seemed to Cashel that the cavalcade of
motor-cars had been moving up the forest roads for many
hours, yet it was still early morning when they stopped at this
hut upon the summit of the range. Seated beside the chauf-
feur in the Buick, Cashel had stared drowsily at the monotonous diorama of shiny undergrowth that flickered past the
windows. Sometimes, for a change, he would look at the
mysterious Aztec profile of the young chaffeur, sometimes at
the pennon that fluttered on the car's bonnet. They were on
their way to the North Shore, to bathe.

The sun was melting the last mists along the Laventille
Hills as the party left Government House that morning, but
up here the mists had not dissolved. Bluish wisps hung about
the forest tree-tops, and only a faint effulgence behind layers
of white cloud showed that there was, somewhere, a sun. The
sky pressed upon the earth—instead of the usual serene
pavilion, it seemed a flat grey lid above their heads. The air
was damp, and distinctly chilly. Puddles of mud blotched the
road on which the cars were parked. A log roof supported on
tree-trunk uprights, and without proper walls, the rest-house
was cold and could have been windy. In it were some dusty
board benches and some tables made of amputated logs. Up
in the dingy corners of its rafters giant spiders had spun their
woollen webs. Within twenty yards of the rest-house a wall
of primeval forest rose.

When he had eaten some eggs Cashel began to wander
down the roadway by which the cars had come. On one side
of the road the hill dropped down into a wide valley, and he

could look out over mile upon mile of coloured tree-tops. How unkempt was this panoply of tropical Nature ! How anonymous and how lacking in style ! He gazed upon the splendid prospect with distaste, and crossed to the other side of the road. Here, in what you could have called a hedgerow, grew many varieties of coarse leaves, like dock-leaves, that looked infinitely poisonous. There were pink sensitive plants and tiny scarlet flowers, and freckled grasses around which hovered woodwasps of abnormal size. No naturalist, Cashel felt at some disadvantage. How much one missed by not being an expert ; all the detail of the world passed you by ; and you were left only with large and often erroneous impressions. He stooped to pick a little bouquet of the grasses, to find them sharp as rapier blades. Further on there were ferns of great elegance, like tufts of plumes upon a Walter Scott helmet. Some of these he gathered, and leaving the road stepped across the grasses and the sensitive plants to the very edge of the forest. Here he hesitated in apprehension, and with a wish to prolong that delicious moment that separates innocence from experience, and gives an added savour to the act of knowing. He had never before been into the forest ; and when he entered it at length he did so suddenly, holding his breath. With hardly a glance to left or right he plunged on and then, stopping, he looked about him. It was a silent submarine world that had received him. He felt submerged in a tank of green light. On all sides the tree-trunks towered above him ; the dimensions of the universe had changed and he seemed nothing but a little doll. Thick lianes and parasites hung from the branches in sculptural festoons. Fan-shaped palm leaves, like those in the Botanic Garden but far more sinister, peeped at him from between smooth-barked trunks. He had never felt so watched, so unisolated in his life. This ominous, resentful scenery would have been entirely frightening, had it not been for the smell. Primeval forests, Cashel discovered, smell like an English rhododendron shrubbery after rain.

There were noises of intrusion in the forest, this morning of

December 1869. The aromatic air crackled with slight unusual sounds, crisper than the sweet hollow bird-notes, more impatient than the slow sonorous falling of some rotted bough. Two men were, in fact, scrambling along in the half-light, groping their way past the great tree-roots ; midgets against the trees' trunks that were russet and ochre and olive-green and black and palest grey. The foliage of these trees was up aloft, a green maze too distant to perceive in detail, for many of the trees were more than one hundred feet high. In the dank mould of the forest soft grave-pits showed where trees once grew and had fallen as they stood and been obliterated by a swift vegetable decay. Here and there in the course of that morning the two men had come upon one of the sudden, miniature clearings that dapple the dark forest, shafts of gay sunshine in which the scarlet plumage of the tree called Prince of Wales's feathers float ; and droop. But chiefly they had gone in the penumbra, hacking at stubborn lianes with their cutlasses, struggling to avoid the wicked *croc-chien* that sprung, a whip of brambles, at your face. They had examined the cannibal creeper, Malapato, the grey parasite that throttles the forest trees. They had plucked specimens of the Brin-villiers plant (much used in local murders) which grew wildly underfoot. Vampire bats had passed them on their skinny wings, and once an unwieldy, darkling Morphou moth had glided noiselessly by. Then they had found a patch of ground that was strewn with shiny green leaves fading to a brilliant crimson, and the guide had pointed upwards in excitement to the stem of a nearby tree. It was Balata, the crimson-leaved, the king of the forest, the tropical woodman's pride. He hacked affectionately at its madder trunk with his knife, and a white blood oozed from the wound. At sight of this pheno-mena his companion, a tall clerical individual with a brow vertically furrowed, who carried a mackintosh, a botany box and a pair of field-glasses, became more animated. Gutta percha ? From the King of the Forest ? The stuttering voice was low-keyed with awe, for here was one of the things he had come to see. The mere fact of standing at last in the primeval forests was enough to go to one's head, for this was

Tropical Forest

Brimstone Hill, St. Kitts, 1837

[*From a water-colour by Lieut. Caddy, R.A.*]

the scenery described so temptingly by Bates and Gosse and Schomburgk ; here were the tree-trunks that looked like Durham Cathedral pillars : there were the orchids riding high which Darwin had discussed in his impressive work on Fertilisation. Who was this zealous disciple, this elderly enthusiast ? Who but Charles Kingsley, the Rector of Eversleigh, the Canon of Chester, that advanced thinker who had shocked his world by writing *Yeast* and had flogged up its dormant patriotism by writing *Westward Ho !*

With his daughter as travelling companion, Canon Kingsley had sailed for Trinidad in December 1869. He went as the guest of one of his many intimate admirers, Mr. Arthur Hamilton-Gordon, the son of Lord Aberdeen and at that moment Governor of Trinidad. Charles Kingsley was only fifty years old, yet he looked and felt far older, for by flaring enthusiasms he had burned his life away. His zest for living was almost insatiable, and it was this attractive characteristic that made him so beloved. His intellectual faculties were of a strangely undistinguished order, and few of his books, letters or sermons contain much that would pass for thought to-day. In him warmth of character went with tetchiness and intolerance ; his sensibility, which was deep, he marred by an unpardonable vulgarity that led him to call George Eliot a concubine, Cardinal Newman a liar and Edmund Campion a prurient priest. But if we cannot now read *Westward Ho !* with interest or pleasure, and find in his private letters views that are as comic as they are distasteful to the adult mind, much must be forgiven to the author of the *Water-Babies* and the *Wonders of the Sea-shore*. These simple books will always please ; and with them his third, but now less widely-known, work on Natural History, *At Last, or a Christmas in the West Indies*. This solid description of seven weeks in Trinidad is written with admirable feeling and sound knowledge. The attitude of persistent appreciation (one of the most tedious in the world ?) may cloy a little, but no one can question the book's high place in the imperial literature of England. He writes of the forests, the flowers and the sky, of the beaches, the savannahs, the palmitos and the rain ; of negroes and creoles and white officials ; of sunsets and sugar-estates ; of sea-weed and sea-shells.

Cashel had picked his way through this book, enviously. Beside the warm-blooded excitement of this invalid clergyman his own reactions seemed especially thin.   As the car bumped down the hills to Blanchisseuse that morning he thought of Kingsley who had made the same long journey on horseback just seventy years before.   Like Kingsley he could look on the shore-grapes and the yellow Mahaut, the green mountains and the plunging foam.   Deliberately he wandered to the mouth of the little river Yarra, where Kingsley's horse had waded in the water that trickles to the sea over the sand.   The afternoon turned hot, the sea-water glittered in the sun.   Cashel crossed the river, and walked on down the long, long beach of white palm-bordered sand.   He felt more than usually forlorn and unmischievous.   Nothing seemed funny any more.   The pompous cars, the rigid tenour of official life, the eccentricity of tropical nature, the beastliness of the heat left him unmoved. He felt suddenly unable to throw cold glances of dislike at the palm-trees.   He forgot to shrink from the sun.   He was soon to leave Trinidad, and the West Indies, and already a cloud of nostalgia was gathering in his mind.   In this late summer of 1939 rumours of war had penetrated to Trinidad. The misspelt messages that came from Reuters over the ticker-tape told of feverish preparations in London and Berlin. Out here too practical steps had been taken for defence.   In the big dining-room of Government House, though the fans still whirred and the footmen handed the dishes, topics of conversation had changed.   People now spoke of defending the oilfields and asked if the Germans would send submarines into the Gulf.   To Cashel this form of talk was no more stimulating than the earlier variety.   Submarines were of no greater interest to him than motor-cars and he knew (if possible) less about them.   But this change of subject added to his general melancholy and made him feel, but in a new way, alien.   It increased his habit of retrospection, until his employers suspected that he took no vestige of interest in them or their present at all.   There was no one to whom he could explain his position, nor did he feel that it deserved tolerance and sympathy. He reflected that if he had been Charles Kingsley he would have welcomed the submarines with a shout of delight—but then he would have welcomed everything else as well. Government House could have been taken for granted : the dances, the dinners, the staircase and the fans. His improbable existence would have seemed entirely convincing. As it was he lived in a dream-world, moving about the high white rooms with the unconsciousness of a somnambulist. For him reality still lay between the pages of the books the Archbishop had lent him. The earnest purpose of Mrs. Carmichael, Trollope's joviality, Dudley's curiosity, the integrity of Sir Hans Sloane, the exuberance of Henry Coleridge, the enthusiasm of Charles Kingsley : he lacked all of these. Beside these living, rounded characters he felt like a flat figure snipped out of a sheet of paper. They had each drawn mental sustenance and emotional excitement from their life in the West Indies. Each had absorbed vital experiences and had described them in a book. As he stood under a palm-tree by the mouth of the Yarra river, gazing out at the foaming South Atlantic that heaved in the tropical sun, Cashel wondered what kind of a book he might produce if he followed these eminent examples. A few descriptive sketches, written without love, without understanding, offered to the reader diffidently—but with a wry smile ?

The cocoa-nut tree by which he was standing cast a thin and crooked shadow on the sand. The rippling waters of the Yarra river twinkled in the sunshine. Far along the beach small emerald waves flopped fussily over black rocks. Cashel turned from the shadow, the river and the sea-shore to the hills that rose cone over cone behind him. Was it all as meaningless as it seemed to him at that moment ? Had he really wasted this single summer spent in Trinidad ?